WRITE HOME ABOUT THIS

"Very well written and easily understood. A must read for junior and senior Service Members alike."
Joe Hannings, *former Sgt. US Marine Corps*

"A thought provoking read that opens your eyes to undiscovered opportunities and a feeling of financial control."
Dyana Baurley, *Agent with New York Life*

WRITE HOME ABOUT THIS

"Educational but also motivational with many important life lessons that everyone can benefit from. The book is well organized and very succinct, while not containing any useless information. The book is able to easily define and explain tough concepts that are critical to understand in the business or stock market world. I would recommend this book to anyone who is either already an entrepreneur or market veteran or even someone who is completely new to the space."

Kevin Byrne, *Regulatory Analyst at Financial Industry Regulatory Authority (FINRA)*

"This book gives every Service Member's warrior mindset a much-needed wealth creation mindset."

Brian Jackson, *former SSgt. USMC*

"A real and genuine portrayal of what one man will do to not only survive but THRIVE in all aspects of his life and career. This is a book you will constantly go back to reference when making any decision. It's a keeper!"
Megan McMullen, *Environmental Protection Agency Contract Specialist*

"As a novice investor, David's book not only helped me with strategy and general knowledge but inspired me to grow my portfolio and more closely monitor potential trade opportunities."
Michael McNelis, *VP of Development – Lease Up*

"Quick read, easy to comprehend, interesting concepts, good stats."
Ravineel Francis, *former US Air Force Mission Support Flight Commander*

WRITE HOME ABOUT THIS

"Perfectly formatted for an everyday dose of intelligence, honesty, and humility. This book is a go-to not just for Service Members, but any individual looking to gain power through knowledge. Inspired me to look beyond my everyday abilities to cultivate awareness and under-standing. Wonderfully written David!"

Michele Evans, *Government Services Administration Contract Specialist*

"This book was inspiring and exciting to me, especially the sections on options. As a commodities trader, I am using these tools to enhance my trading. I believe it is a safer approach and lowers my risk while trading commodities."

Hector Cordero, *SL Trading*

The riches you may enjoy.

Edited by Jill C. Dalin

To my very understanding wife Megan.

Love, Dave

Courtesy of

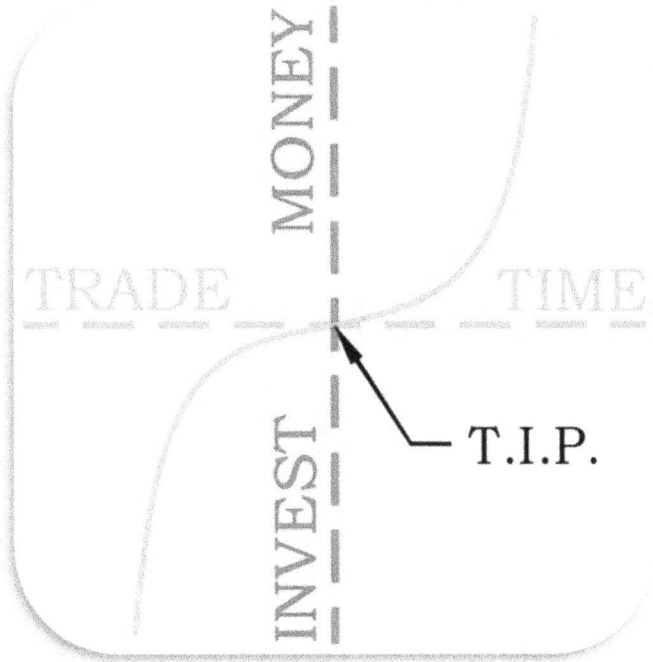

The Inflection Point

Where Trading Meets Investing ™

T.I.P. Inc.

Vision

To give Service Members
World-Class Market
Education

Mission

To get our content into the
hands of every Veteran
seeking employment and
every Service Member
serving overseas

CHAPTER MAP

(TABLE OF CONTENTS)

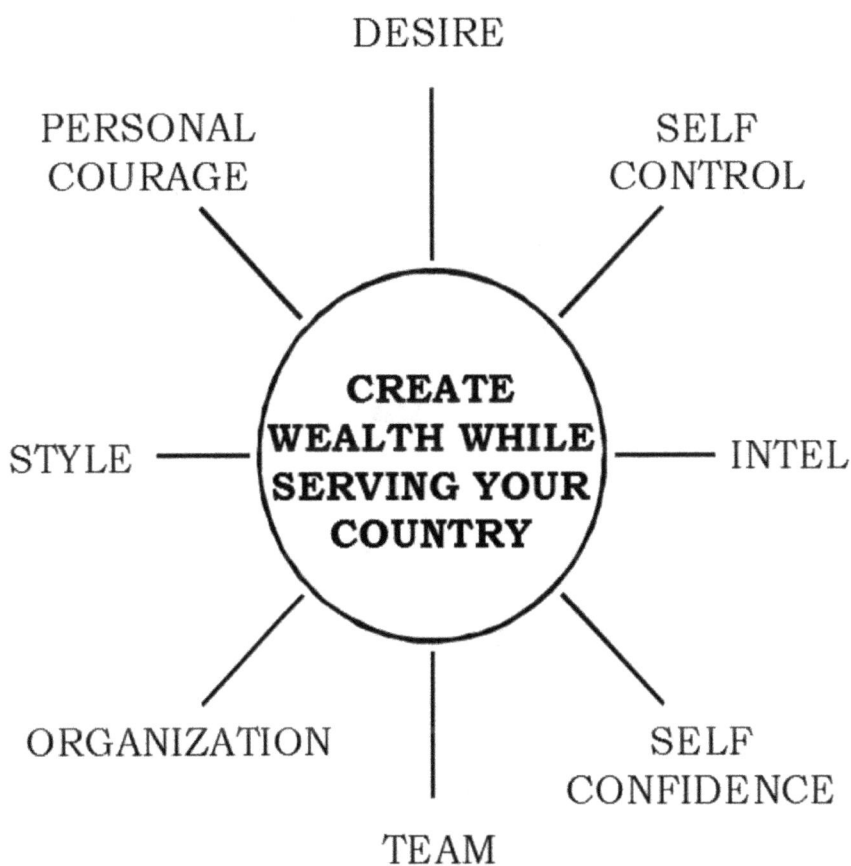

DESIRE

PERSONAL
COURAGE

SELF
CONTROL

STYLE

**CREATE
WEALTH WHILE
SERVING YOUR
COUNTRY**

INTEL

ORGANIZATION

SELF
CONFIDENCE

TEAM

When I arrived at Bagram Air Field circa 2011, I had no idea what to expect. Mostly everyone at the office said I'd be sitting at a desk doing 'on-base' engineering. Something told me not to believe that, and I tried to prepare myself for the worst.

When I finally arrived at my duty station, I checked in with Erasmo, the Resident Engineer from Jacksonville District, who was in charge. We all called him Raz. He was a great leader. He knew exactly what it took to run a team.

Raz had to position me, and thinking back, he was probably slightly nervous about breaking the news that they needed me in the 'off-base' Resident Office. I believe that things happen for a reason- that's just my personality. There is a reason I was there, and there is a reason you are *here*, wherever you happen to be.

So, when Raz told me I would be psyched about my new position, and that I would get to travel out with the security team and take helicopters out to sites, I was genuinely excited. He did a great job helping me to adjust, and I worked on being open-minded enough to be able to handle whatever came my way.

Had I had a different mindset going in, my transition could have turned out to be much less smooth. Raz and I travelled to several sites 'outside the wire' in the following months. Only because of the care, guidance, and protection of you, the Service Members who assisted and guarded us, did we come back in one piece. This book is my way of saying thank you.

During one of those helicopter missions I captured one of Afghanistan's little known gems, Band-e Amir National Park. I felt a need to share the image with you right on the cover of this book. There is beauty to be found even under the most difficult of circumstances.

While you are *here*, you'll be under my full care, guidance, and protection, because this is exactly the treatment I received from you brave Service Members overseas.

We'll start in a way that costs you nothing, so you can only walk away with more than what you have starting out. I genuinely believe that you can, and I want to help you to make 30% profit *and more* every year working part time and remotely from anywhere, with little to no overhead, and no fear your business will become outdated.

I'm going to show you exactly how to strategically position yourself in your chosen market with a scientifically-proven, market-tested plan. As a Service Member, you already have many of the traits required for success. I will repeatedly refer to these traits, because I truly want you succeed.

If you aren't familiar with Star Wars, a *Jedi* is a term for a highly-trained warrior that studies, serves, and uses *the force* to control energy with his or her mind. The power of

suggestion is a Jedi's specialty. I will use the metaphor of the Jedi to help you to internalize a successful mindset and to master any market.

Put your doubts, fears and worries aside for a second. It's true that what happens in the market is beyond our control. We must accept that there are unknowns: both known unknowns and unknown unknowns. If you can remain in control of yourself, and apply the simple techniques in this book, you can profit in any market regardless of events and conditions.

The calmest one in the room is always thinking the clearest.

Peace of mind is what most seek, yet to most, the market represents the furthest thing from that. To gain peace of mind in any market, start by answering the question "Am I a *strategist* or am I a *tactician*?" Few people think of themselves as either. Most of us are tacticians: if you *trade* your time for money, you're a *tactician*. It's easier for a tactician to react, and harder initially to take charge and be proactive.

Only a very small percentage, maybe 2%, are true *strategists*. To create wealth, you need the skills of both the strategist *and* the tactician. When you can combine the skills of both, you catapult to an elite group. This group is much smaller, somewhere in the order of 1 in 1,250. You can think of these few as being similar to the Special Forces of the Military. This elite group *creates* wealth, and controls their market prices.

This book is designed as a step-by-step guide for *creating* your own wealth. If you're good now, this will help to get you to the mastery level with discipline, persistence, and confidence.

We start with *Desire*, because accomplishing anything of great importance requires it. It's the strength of your desire that will ensure persistence and perseverance in your market.

First, I'll shine light on the mental state you need to stay in control. Not all of us are Navy SEALs (If you are, the *Self Control* chapter will resonate with you).

Then, we'll go through the physical transactions of a trade, step-by-step, with a glimpse into the mind of the best traders. Even high frequency trading algorithms can't compete with the professional market master.

Try not to over-think the term market. While we will be discussing the stock market quite a bit, markets involve more than just stocks, commodities, and currencies. Markets also include personal services, products, and *ideas* as well.

In the *Style* chapter, I provide example plans for trading in multiple timeframes that can produce extraordinary gains if applied appropriately. These are useful for foreign currencies (forex) trading and commodities trading as well as stock trading. The foreign currencies and commodities prices are often the root causes of the changes in the equity markets, aka the stock market.

Create your great idea from your imagination. It should flash in your mind, like a muzzle flash in the pitch black. You may not know the full significance of the image yet, but you'll know what it is. What is it you want? Financial freedom? Job independence? By the end of this book, you'll know.

In *Style*, I provide guidelines, checklists, and triggers used by the best educators on Wall Street. You will ultimately be in a position to make the decision on a strategy that suits you and your objectives.

Finally, I'll tie everything together and talk about wealth beyond just making money, because we all know happiness is more than just dollars and cents.

I consider Warren Buffet the greatest investor of our time. He spends <u>80%</u> of his day reading. In his annual shareholder letter, he wrote, "When promised quick profits, respond with a quick 'No'."

"Never invest in a business you don't understand." ~ *Warren Buffet*

CHAPTER I
DESIRE

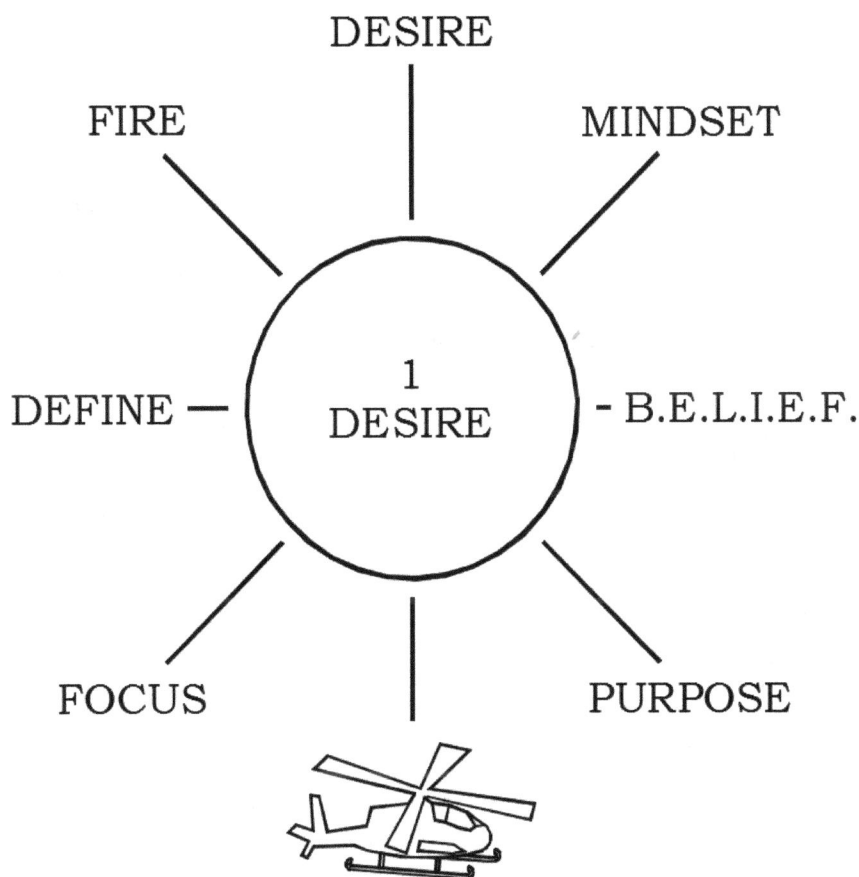

Desire, the first step toward riches…

The first time I met my (now) wife, I *knew* I wanted to get to know her better. I also knew beautiful girls are hard to get to know. Press too hard and you blow it. Don't even try, and you don't have a chance. So, what did I do? I nonchalantly started messaging her to get together for a drink after work. I started out saying I was going out with friends and invited her. First, she responded with "Can't, too busy." Then, "Sorry, not today."

The next week, I invited her to a happy hour. "I need to get my hair done." The following week, "I need to pick up my brother." And then, "I would, but I'm sooooo tired." The week after that, "I'm going out with some friends" (not you though).

Next, I tried just texting just "Hh".

"What's Hh?" she asked.

I remember being relieved. Finally, something other than a rejection, "Happy hour" I replied.

"Nope, not today."

The next day, I tried again - "Hh?" She knew what it meant now. "Super busy, sorry!" (I had a feeling she wasn't super busy or sorry though).

The next day, "Hh?"

She started just replying, "Ahh, can't today." She probably thought, *Is he really going to Happy Hour every day?* Not exactly... but I totally would have if she was going!

The fact that she kept responding gave me this glimmer of hope. Maybe she was trying to figure out whether I was interested or just an alcoholic. "Hh?" I kept asking, each week day, around the same time, for days and days.

"Hh?" was just enough to let her know I was there, simple enough that she got the message right away, short enough that I couldn't screw anything up, and it got her wondering a little bit about me.

"Not today." "Too busy." "Do you do anything else?" From her responses, I could tell she was smart and funny.

"Yes, I do plenty of things, but I'm more interested in what *you* do."

Six months later, I was still texting "Hh?" every week, day after day, rejection after rejection. "Getting my hair done." "Going shopping with my mom." I didn't get upset, even though she wouldn't make any time for me for six months. I knew she was just making excuses, and I didn't care. I just kept trying: "Hh?" Then, one day, my world stopped.

"*Maybe*, where are you going?"

As it turned out, she was sweet like candy and bubbly like champagne. She was perfect. I *knew* she was *the ONE.*

What is it you *really* want? You can get *it,* no matter what *it* is, with the right approach.

How bad do you want *it*? Will you stimulate your mind to get *it*? Love, music, and the attainment of riches are all mind stimuli. Would you believe that termites chew through wood twice as fast listening to heavy metal? I love working out to some classic rock myself.

Yes, drugs and alcohol may stimulate your mind as well. Veterans suffering from Post-Traumatic Stress Disorder or depression are not only more likely to be prescribed painkillers than their peers, they are more prone to over-medicate with painkillers in sometimes deadly combination with psychotropic drugs, especially benzodiazepines. Meanwhile, at the Department of Veteran Affairs, prescriptions for highly addictive painkillers are surging.

Even when painkillers are used as directed, the chances of Veterans becoming dependent after just a few weeks are high. So how do you combat an addiction? Stay connected and engage with others in your community. If you are in a crisis and don't know where to turn, the Veteran Affairs crisis hotline is 1-800-273-8255.

Not everyone wants what you want. Does anyone *really* want drugs? No. However, if you can't find something, *anything* to concentrate on, you begin to drift. Only you can decide what you want or desire. What is the ONE thing you *really* desire? Only about 2% can even answer the question, "What is your *greatest* desire in life?"

Just "money" isn't a strong desire. It is important that your desire is more specific than that. Imagine, for example, a specific amount of money. See if you can imagine the specified amount so clearly that you can feel and act like you have it.

I'm going to convince you that you can get any *ONE* thing you desire by introducing Jedi Mind Tricks (JMT).

Some people lack the *belief* they can get whatever they want by fixating their mind on the object of their desire. The *belief* costs you nothing, so why not *believe*? I truly believe in the next simple mind trick, because it has helped me.

JMT
⊕ *Whatever you can conceive and believe, you can achieve*

Notice the trick says nothing about needing money, needing any education, or anything else. All you need to start is your mind and soul. If you feel what you're doing is right, and you believe in it, then it's time to start conceiving your plan.

There is no "minimum amount" to start conceiving and believing. Your lack of money, or lack of education, doesn't matter. Every time you even think it does, you're hurting yourself. Putting limitations on what you *think* you can do, just doesn't make sense does it?

Tell your mind your one desire, whatever *it* is for you. *It* may be your desire for financial freedom or job independence. Whatever *it* is, repeat *it* over and over every day and *the very thought* will get you closer to *it*.

All the breaks you need in life wait within your imagination...

"Imagination is the workshop of your mind, capable of turning mind energy into accomplishment and wealth." ~ *Napoleon Hill*

In any market, you need to dedicate time to training. Not just training your body, training your mind also. The time spent on training must be continuous and progressive. Take as an example practicing *Organization*. Why is it that the superstars are always doing more? Miss a week, and you're missing something.

Trading in any market requires taking risks. What makes the master different? He *knows* his or her risk. Before risking one actual dollar, you are going to practice on paper so that you will be able to develop a market-tested plan that you have confidence in, irrespective of market conditions. If you can't thrive in a simulated market, you should certainly not trade your hard-earned cash. The key is to trade as if the paper money were REAL. Put out a 100 dollar bill on the table. Make it REAL.

The fact is, one in three traders loses almost everything. *Ouch!* Three out of four options expire worthless. Are you taking advantage of all your options? We'll talk more about your options in _Style_.

If you offer personal services, think of trading paper money as equivalent to collecting money *before* you provide the service. This lowers your risk of losing to zero. Working to sell your product or service before you provide it is a strategic approach to *test the need* for what you are offering. If no one is interested in buying *it*, you can save time, money, and trouble by NOT producing *it*.

The positive **mindset**...

"Whether you think you can, or you think you can't, you're right."
~ *Henry Ford*

Do you think Henry Ford knew how his team of engineers was going to cast the block of an engine in one pour? Why did Mr. Ford desire it? He made a definite decision to demand it from his team. Year after year, the team concluded it was impossible, until one year, through the development of new technology, the team was able to produce it.

Ford was a strategist. The strategist will look out two years and beyond.

The strategist is like the investor; they share a long-view perspective. The tactician may track his or her month-to-month, week-to-week, day-to-day, hour-to-hour, and minute-to-minute. The tactician is similar to the trader; they share a short-term perspective. Both trader and investor have their place in the market, and I'll explain more in _Style_.

Service Members with skills in trading _and_ investing are a rare breed. These Service Members can be twice as effective doing half as much.

Skill at the mastery level requires repeated training, and it's not just any training. It's specific training for whatever you're trying to do.

That means you must be *trying* to get *your ONE thing*. One without the other just won't pay off. Both require a great deal of time and energy and the right amount of pressure to master.

Investing involves strategic planning. If you plan to invest, invest continuously. If you don't want to invest continuously, don't bother investing at all. Spend your time trading in your market instead. Before you invest in someone else's company and vision, spend some time to think about what *your* market is.

My ***B.E.L.I.E.F.***

Beneficial
Energy
Lurks
In
Every
Failure

I believe in the truth represented by this acronym.

The ironic part is just knowing this acronym won't help you. You must *believe* it. It's something you feel in your heart and your soul. Believing in this acronym has the power to change a lifelong disability into a strategic advantage that will change your world from a slum to a paradise. Powerful and mighty is the human mind.

Definite major **purpose**...

Your single largest driving *force* is
your definite major purpose. When
you act with purpose, you get what
you want. Purpose is strong enough
to awaken *the force* within you. It's
obvious Service Members have
purpose.

Freedom: all Americans want
freedom.

> *JMT*
> ⊕ *You don't accept what you don't
> desire*

Take away the *idea* of freedom, as
imagined by our forefathers, and
perhaps there would have been no
revolution. Redefine your purpose
with greater meaning.

I believe everyone was put on this earth for a purpose. Don't hesitate to reach out to me and share your story. The trends you create today can set into motion unbelievable life accomplishments.

There will inevitably be losses and failures on your journey to wealth. Yes, it sucks. There's nothing anyone can say or do to change that fact. Instead, examine your current position in the moment and think of your potential risk given your historical losses.

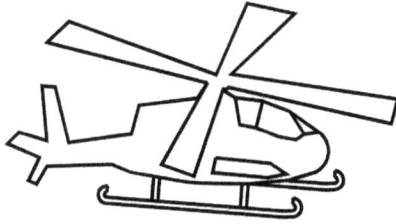

Shoot down your **helicopters**…

Charlie Wilson was the driving force behind the Russian exit from Afghanistan during the Cold War. In the movie *Charlie Wilson's War*, Tom Hanks, portraying Wilson, does a great job of illustrating single-minded purpose and using failure as a means to figure out the path to success.

The US was faced with the problem of Afghan civilians getting slaughtered by Russian helicopters. In scene after scene, Wilson (Hanks) repeats the same thing to the weapons experts and to the politicians, "If we could just *shoot down those damn helicopters*, everything would start going our way."

In the end, that is exactly what happens. Charlie leads Operation Cyclone, the largest ever CIA mission, to arm the Afghan mujahideen with surface-to-air missiles and they shoot down the helicopters. We'll rocket back to Charlie Wilson's War in *Team*.

Concentrate on your game-changing statement, and define *your* metaphorical helicopters.

Define your loftiest goals...

Thinking small or vague will hinder your ability to progress. Your limitations are basically the ones you allow to be limitations in your mind. When you *know* your ONE true desire, your purpose, you *know* it's big *and* specific.

JMT

⊕ *Your goals are* **BIG** *and specific*

Write down what you are prepared to give in return for your big and specific goal. Think of the commitment of time you are going to block off. It takes the same time and money to think big as it does to think small, so why not think big?

You may not know *exactly* how to scale up and we'll get to that in _Personal Courage_. Block off a set amount of time to just think.

Focus on details like space, time, and strategy. Think of how you will keep track of your progress.

Focus...

Focus on one thing at a time. There is study after study proving that multi-taskers actually get LESS done. Try to do too much and end up with less. Pick one thing to do at a time. This ensures you get something done.

It takes the same amount of effort to concentrate on something big than to concentrate on something small.

When your focus can stretch no more, you will need to call on superstars. Phone a friend, call thousands of mentors. In Chapter Five, we will show you how to concentrate on building your _Team_.

Many people get stuck working _in_ their business instead of _on_ their business. What is the single greatest barrier between you and your greatest desire? Email it to me. Maybe I can help. I love challenges.

Fire of desire...

A burning desire mixed with enduring faith has a funny way of becoming reality. If you quit at the first objection, or the first thousand objections, you lack faith and will find it difficult to reach your goal.

JMT
⊕ *Burn your boats so you are forced to take the island*

You'll never give up: that's what faith does. You are past thinking you won't get it, you *think* and *know* you will, and you can see yourself with *it*. If you are going to do anything, do it better than anyone.

Whatever your calling in life, just be the best you can be.

"If a man is called to be a street sweeper, he should sweep streets as even as a Michelangelo painted, or Beethoven composed music, or Shakespeare wrote poetry. He should sweep streets so well that all the hosts of heaven and earth will pause to say, here lived a great street sweeper who did his job well."

~*Martin Luther King*

CHAPTER II
SELF CONTROL

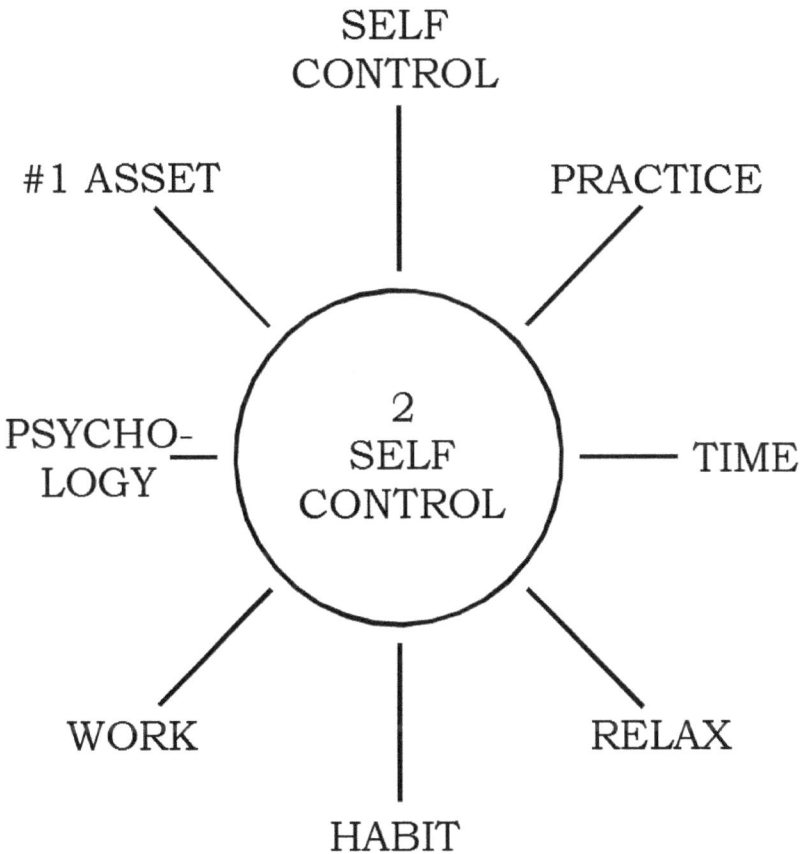

SELF
CONTROL

#1 ASSET

PRACTICE

PSYCHO-
LOGY

2
SELF
CONTROL

TIME

WORK

RELAX

HABIT

I can't teach you **self control**...

Self control comes from within. Once you get to the mastery level of skill through repetition, it takes self control to hammer the final nail in the coffin. You need self control to start, and you'll need it much more to finish.

JMT
  ⊕ *Control your mind first, and your body will follow*

Self control starts by controlling your thoughts. If you're thinking the right thing, it's only a matter of time before you can control yourself enough to act on those thoughts. Find out the weak spots in your thoughts, and start thinking differently.

Compare yourself to others achieving more success. You can always learn something from someone doing it better. Block off time to master self control early or pay the price later. We are all given the same amount of time, why is it that some of us get to the mastery level, while others never do?

Practice, practice, practice…

When you find your area of expertise, concentrate on mastering the skills needed for the position. Don't do 12,000 different things four times. Do four things 12,000 times. Once you get to the mastery level of skill, this alone will increase your returns.

To be a master is to be a professional. In Malcolm Gladwell's book "Blink," he explains professionalism to a T.

'Professional jam tasters' were compared to a random control group. These two groups were asked to taste test common jams like Smuckers and compare them to other brands and no-name jams.

In the first round, each group was only asked to rate the jams on a certain number scale from best to worst. Not surprisingly, the two groups, professional and non-professional, rated the jams about the same.

For the second round of sampling, the same two groups were asked to rate the same twelve jams; however, this time they had to also make comments on specific features (i.e. texture, consistency, origin of ingredients). The professional tasters could rate the jams the same. However, the non-professionals changed their minds about the best overall jam when required to analyze and assign a rating to specific features of each jam. This is the exact reason professionals get paid more. M

Former Navy SEAL Brandon Webb, cites maturity and the ability to be a steady operator as the qualities required for success on high-stakes sensitive missions in his book "The 21st Century Sniper."

M Malcolm Gladwell, *Blink,* 2005

Ask yourself, "Do I spend time thinking about how I execute?" The ability to execute flawlessly and to do so consistently in any market makes you the master.

Is **time** your #1 constraint?

Why is it that some can accomplish greatness, while others complain there is not enough time in the day?

Superstars have schedules that go out months for a reason. Missed appointments can cost thousands or maybe even millions! We are all given the same amount of time, yet some choose to achieve well beyond what most agree is impossible. Time is only a constraint when not controlled and directed.

Work smarter, not harder. Every single day we are faced with similar decisions. What do I wear today? Do I have any important meetings at work or outside of work? Can I think about the order of things while doing thoughtless daily activities, like showering or brushing my teeth?

Relax...

Don't forget to add time on your calendar dedicated to relaxing and spending time with those important to you. You need this time to rest your mind. Use the time to tell your body to heal. Set aside time to meditate. If you feel stressed, think of your block of relaxation time.

Habits make you; you make habits…

A **habit** takes at least a month or two to create. If you do something 15 days in a row, on the sixteenth day, it will not be any easier. It won't feel like a habit, nor will it stick without further effort. Most of the energy required to create the habit will be spent in the first month. Getting into a habit is like shooting a rocket into outer space. There is a gravitational force that wants to pull you back to your old ways, that is, until you get into orbit. Calculate your escape velocity before buying any rocket parts.

Get in a habit of maintaining an open mind to all people and in all situations. The costliest thing in any organization is the closed-mindedness of the people that work there. Being closed toward others, closed to opportunities, and closed to *ideas* stifles your personal growth, and hurts your success and the success of your company.

Psychology isn't everything, or is it?

The market is very good at getting you to make the wrong decision. You need 100% confidence in your strategy. Stick to your market-tested, scientifically-proven plan.

Fast price movements upward can trigger the 'Fear of Missing Out' feeling; however, this feeling shouldn't trigger your finger. Resist the urge. Treat making a trade as serious as you would firing a weapon. You can't get that bullet back.

Every Service Member is fully capable of envisioning him or herself in someone else's boots. Sometimes it helps to have an out-of-body experience to *sense* possible solutions for your so-called "impossible" problems.

You are your **#1 asset**...

Your most valuable asset is you. Your time is invaluable. The power of your mind is infinite. Every Service Member carries the ability to control and direct his or her mind to whatever ends he or she desires. There is a reason you landed in the job you are in. There is a reason you have *this* book.

If you struggle with any task, look to the *greatest of all time* and study how that task was accomplished. Don't sell yourself; control and educate yourself. Don't be afraid to reach out to me, so I can help you find the greatest of all time in your industry. I've found that by helping others, I am helping myself.

CHAPTER III
INTEL

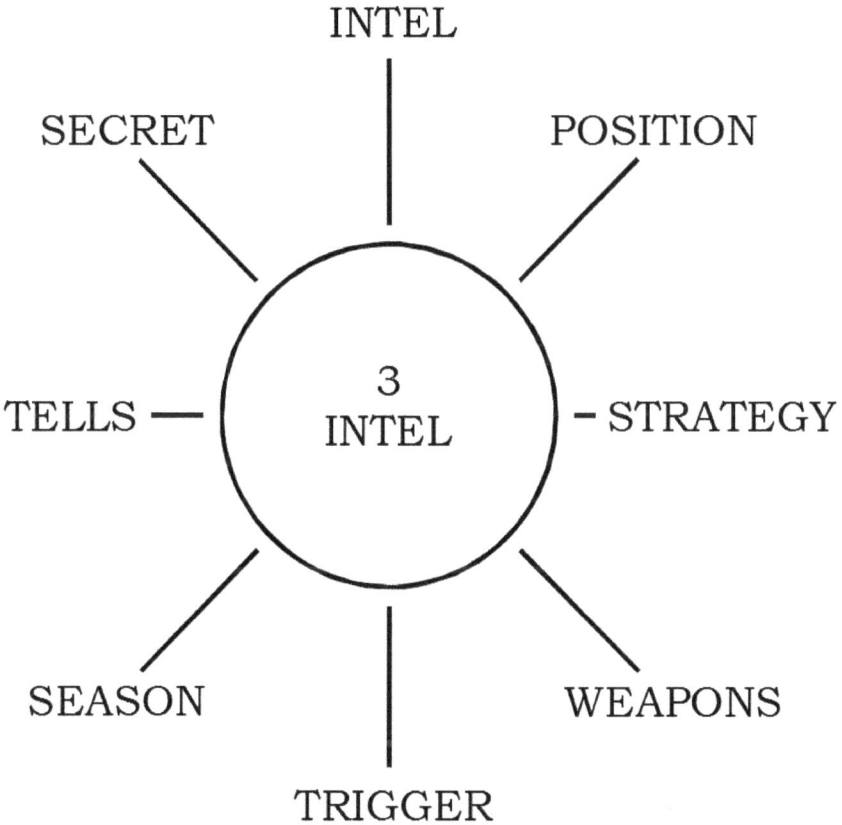

Intel is receiving useful information without violating the rights of others.

Whatever field you're in, there is always knowledge floating in the airwaves in the form of information. Receiving this information may spawn opportunity.

Check your **position**...

In a gunfight, position is everything. Bulletproof Hesco barriers and bulletproof vests could save your life. Choose the safest position with the best angle shot, right?

In the real world, and in the combat world, rarely do you get to pick your location. Usually, you are told to go. However, just because you are in a dangerous location, doesn't mean you can't choose a position of power.

No doubt, in the moment, you need to track closely your entries in to and exits out of enemy territory. Take note of dangers, and avoid high risk areas if possible. If you're caught in a sticky situation, your ability to navigate the hazards will determine your survival.

Take inventory of your assets. Know the closest exit, impenetrable objects, and exposed areas. The more aware you are of your position, the better your chances of escaping alive.

So you survived the battlefield, and you want to take the position concept to the real world. Great idea! In the real world, you are in control of your position at all times (unless you're in jail; sorry OJ, maybe next year).

You need as much courage in business as you do in battle. Bankruptcy is probably the greatest fear in the business world. But you can think of bankruptcy as a reset on your finances, a second life. Bankruptcy sounds bad, however when compared to death, it sounds like a good alternative. There is no shame in bankruptcy. Walt Disney went bankrupt two times before he succeeded in building his wealth-creation empire.

How do you plant yourself in your industry and sector *so deep* that you get the sort of top-of-mind awareness that someone like Disney had?

Define your ultimate strategic position as spelled out in your plan. Actual examples of plans are given in _Style_. These examples are meant to be a guide: everyone thinks and operates differently.

Mastering any market requires consistent time and discipline to track price movements carefully over specific periods of time. In this chapter, I'm going to reference the stock market, to give ideas on how you can profit with low risk. There are many moving parts, and I'm about to dismantle the engine to show you how the market is designed, piece by piece.

Your success rate varies drastically whether you rely upon mentors or not. We'll talk more about mentors in _Team_. The science behind your trade plan requires the level of math of a fifth grader. You just need to find someone teaching fifth grade math, and be open minded enough to create an outside-the-box, strategic approach.

Strategy is your advantage...

When you see a chart of the market on TV, it will usually show a single line denoting price movement. This line is drawn from connecting the close price of specified time periods. It took me losing a lot of real money for me to examine this price action with a magnifying glass. What I found is there is always a _range_ of market prices. To see the range in its entirety, you need to pull up a *candlestick* chart.

You can find the candlestick charts on Stockcharts.com or Finviz.com.

These candlesticks break down time periods by week, day, 15 minute intervals, five minute intervals, and even one minute intervals. I'll go more into timeframe in the *Style* chapter.

The Japanese perfected these candles as an easy way to visualize price movement over time.

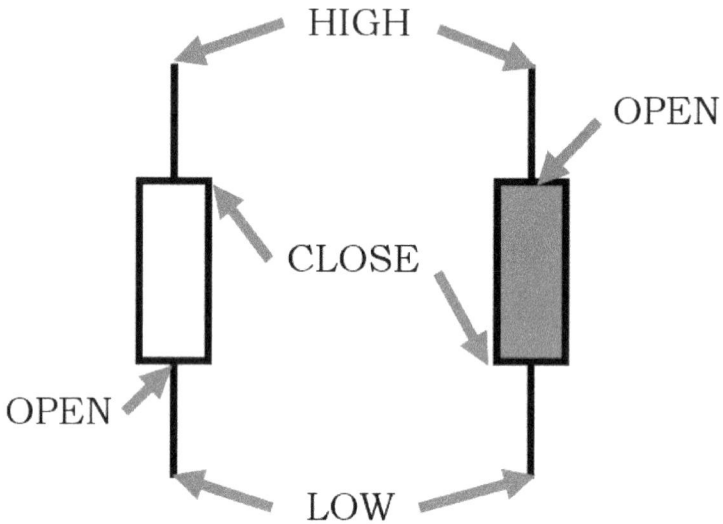

Bullish candle   Bearish candle
(Price goes up)   (Price goes down)

The candlestick on the left represents a period of positive gain, while the right candlestick represents a period where the price fell. Trading without using candlesticks is equivalent to using a Sniper Rifle without a scope.

Each candlestick, or period, graphically displays four key

numbers for traders. The rectangular body represents everything in between the open and close price. The lines (or wicks) extending above and below the body define the trading period highs and lows, respectively.

An average true range (ATR) is the range a stock is expected to move based on the historical period highs and lows. The default period number is commonly found as the average of the last fourteen periods.

Traders use the ATR to set stop-loss levels and targets. If you enter a position, you don't want normal price fluctuations to cause your stop-loss to trigger. I see good traders set stop-losses that are at least one ATR below the entry price.

Volatility is the measure of how liable something is to experience rapid and unpredictable change. More volatile stocks will have higher *percentage* average true ranges in relation to the underlying security price.

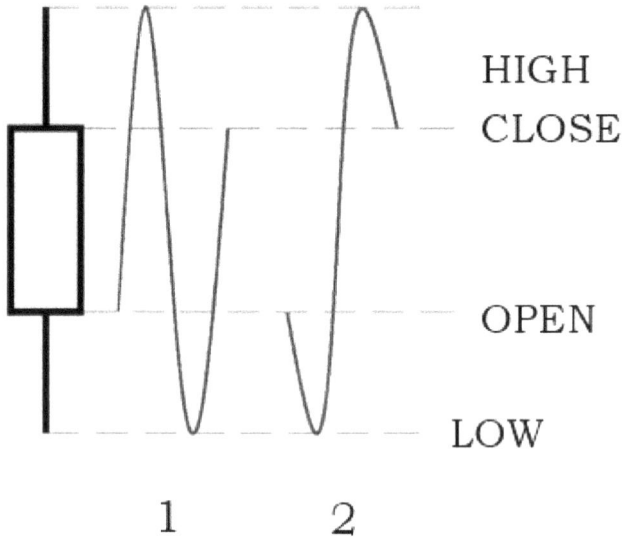

The movement of the bullish candle will experience a wave like 1 or 2. Which one, you won't know by just seeing the candle. However, the key points are the high and the low. These are levels you will want to keep track of for price breakouts.

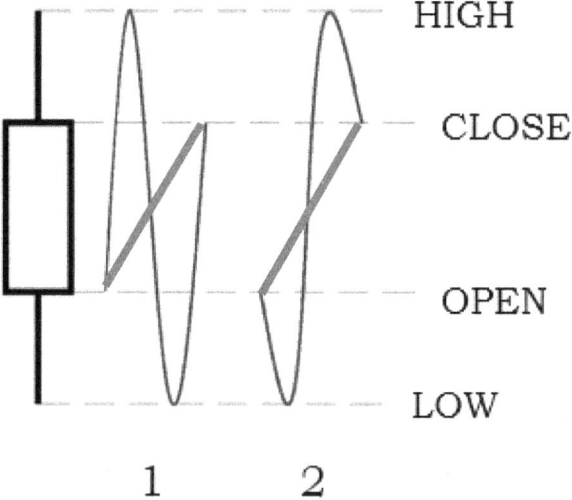

When you draw a line from open to close, both 1 and 2 look the same. However, it's clear you are missing half of the movement.

JMT
   ⊕ *You follow the candlesticks*

These candlesticks flow side by side in real-time, so you can visualize the actual range of the movement. Combinations of candlesticks may alert you to certain chart patterns that are scientifically-proven to have a higher probability of a certain price movement.

Trading *is* gambling, with one important exception. You can't get banned from the market if you're on a hot streak. What the risk-adverse love to ignore is the fact we risk death every single day we wake up. There is no way of avoiding *risk* itself.

There are, however, ways to minimize your risk by examining your positions and calculating your exposure. When gambling in any market, if you want to gamble *as long as you live*, you need the odds at least slightly in your favor. The idea is to *be the casino,* not the degenerate gambler.

If you aren't tracking your win/loss percentages, risk-to-reward ratios, and probabilities, you won't know where you are going wrong. I offer some tools in <u>Style</u> and our trade templates are free to Military and Veterans.

High probability outcomes are just that. There are no guarantees in life, and anyone who tells you otherwise is lying. If you trade, you are bound to lose. The idea is to win more than you lose, and never put yourself in the position to take a catastrophic loss.

Have you heard of the *Devil's Wager?*

*The Devil fans five cards, one of which you must choose. You know four of the five cards are aces, and you know the other is a two. The devil **forces you** to choose ONE card; but before you choose, you need to guess what card you will pick. If you guess correctly, you receive one billion dollars; if you guess incorrectly, your soul is his. So, what do you guess?*

?

Most will try to avoid answering, because they fear the outcome. Even though there is nothing to lose, I have still had people refuse to answer, even after pressing them.

The correct guess in this situation is an ace because there is an 80% chance (4 out of 5) that that is the card you will choose.

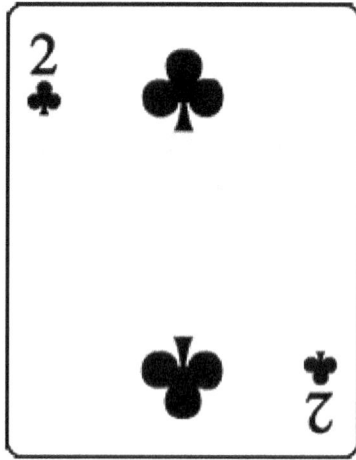

So, you pull a 2. Did you guess incorrectly? NO. If you guessed an ace, you guessed *correctly*. You used your intel to make the best possible decision in the moment.

If you went through life betting against the odds every time, you bank account would be much closer to zero. *Force yourself* to make a trade, even a trade only on paper, and you will quickly see the skills you need to profit in your chosen market.

The answers lie in the statistics and hard numbers built on solid facts. Most market experts swear by certain 'technical indicators' for entries and exits, however only a small percentage of them actually make a profit. The real experts swear by certain strategies because those are the triggers in *their* plan.

It's dangerous to just pick up and use someone else's plan. Try to understand why it's working and see if you can find a way to bring that information into harmony with your own _Style_.

Use **patterns** to sharpen your axe...

The patterns become weapons with training. Just like real weapons, these weapons can do more harm than good if not used properly. In the market, there are common patterns with more probable outcomes. Statistically, this is the way to gain an edge in your market, from the tactical side of your entry. Your probability of success jumps higher when you use these secret weapons to execute your trade entries and exits.

To arbitrarily say any one of these candlestick combinations will have a precise 60% to 40% probability doesn't make sense. Every trade is situational. I can say with certainty that there are patterns that do have a more probable outcome. We are going to focus on four, keeping in mind all trades are situational.

You wouldn't try to use a sniper rifle at close range, or rip your M16 at a target 500 yards out. Trading is similar, in that you want to use the weapon that fits your situation.

Weapon#1: The hammer

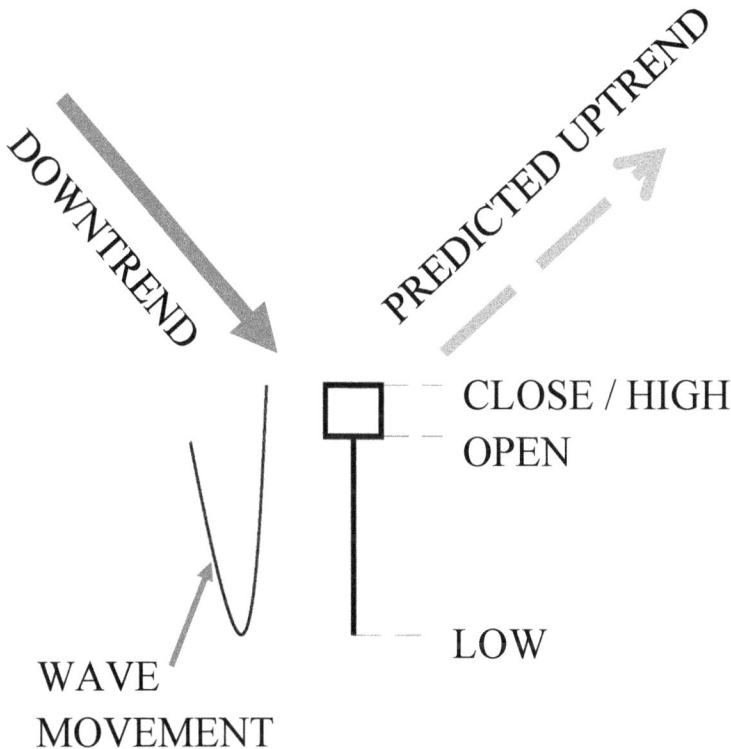

DOWNTREND

PREDICTED UPTREND

CLOSE / HIGH
OPEN

LOW

WAVE
MOVEMENT

For the hammer candle to be reliable, the price movement needs to be in an extended downtrend occurring over many periods. The close price in the hammer candle will also be the period high. Study the wave movement to understand the theory behind this weapon. With only one reversal in the hammer candle, the movement is only showing half of a sine wave pattern. Therefore, you can expect to see a continuation of the upward movement to complete the wave.

Sine Wave pattern

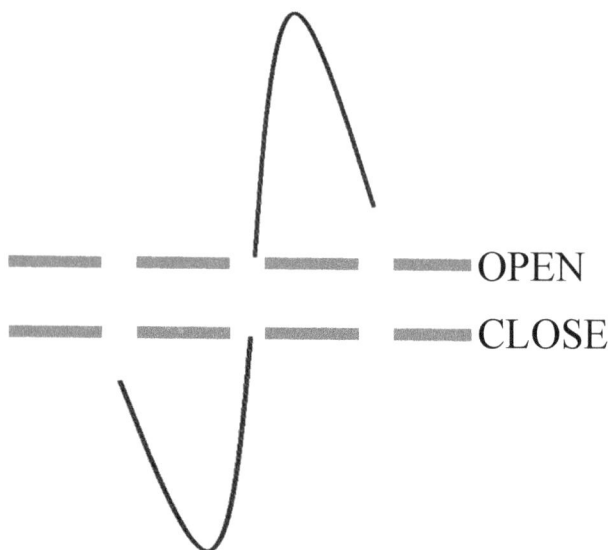

OPEN

CLOSE

Weapon #2: The kicker

This is my favorite and most reliable pattern. The next figure is a bullish (think prices moving higher) kicker.

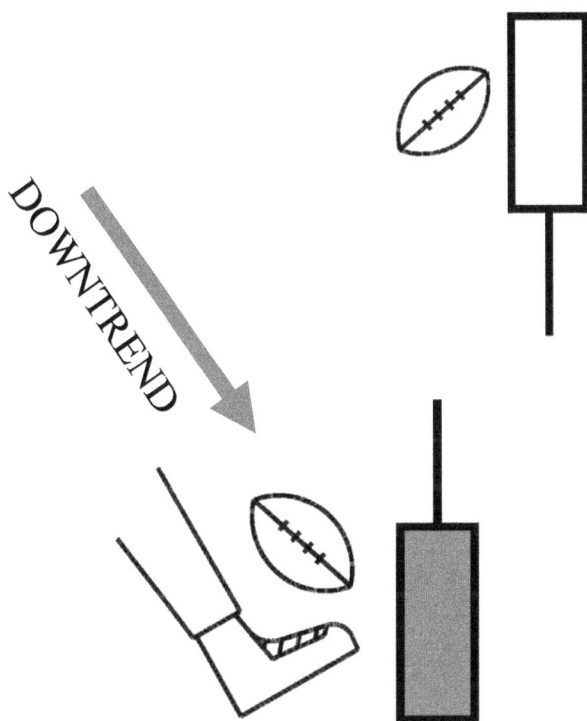

When the downward movement occurs first, think of it as being similar to the football being dropped before being punted. In the next frame, you see the ball in the air. When you see a kicker, you are catching the middle of the upward momentum.

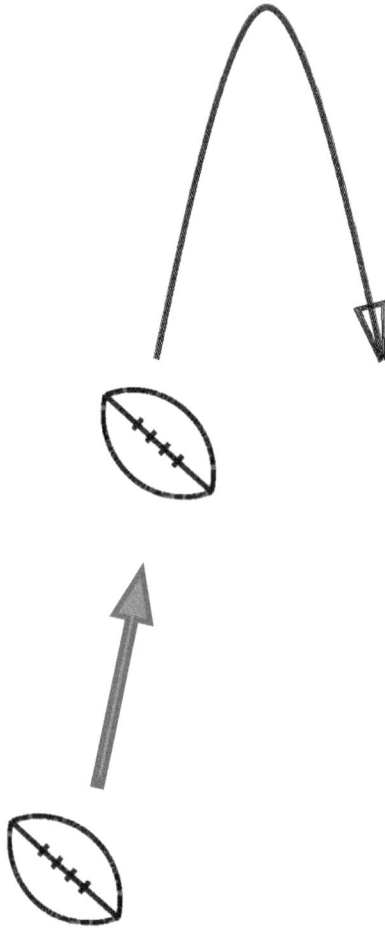

Based on experience, the probability of a move higher after a bullish kicker is about seven in ten, or seventy percent.

So why do I have faith in my *kicker*? It creates a *gap* in the sine wave, effectively cutting the chord on any previous patterns. The resistance has turned to support. The bigger the gap, the greater energy wave to expect.

It's the momentum that carries the stock higher, like the split second the ball is kicked up. Earnings releases, company announcements, and market news may all cause *gaps* in prices. Whatever the reason, it *forces* a reevaluation of the price by the market makers. Market makers are the ones in the pits doing this for a living. The market makers have real money on the line. They try *really* hard to get the price right.

JMT
    ⊕ *You trust the market prices*

Weapon #3: Flat top breakout

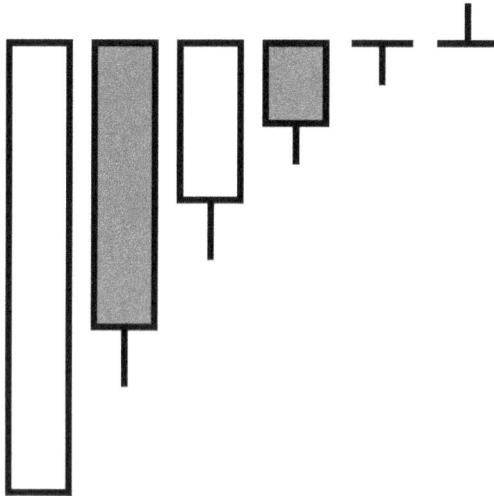

Consolidation occurs with higher lows building up to a clear line of resistance. Imagine the sine waves getting smaller. The price range continually shrinks from day to day. This causes energy to build up, like shaking a bottle of champagne. Wait for a pop, then get your glass ready.

I've seen success in using a previous candle's high as a trigger to enter a bullish position. A logical first target would be the high of day.

Weapon #4: The bull flag

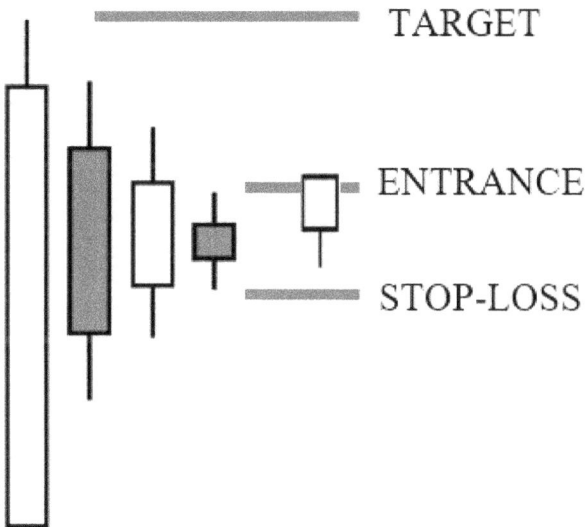

You want the distance from your entrance to your target to be double the distance from your entrance to your stop-loss. The golden rule of trading is a risk-to-reward ratio of 2 to 1.

Let's dissect the bull flag. The first two candles are a great example of a *retracement.*

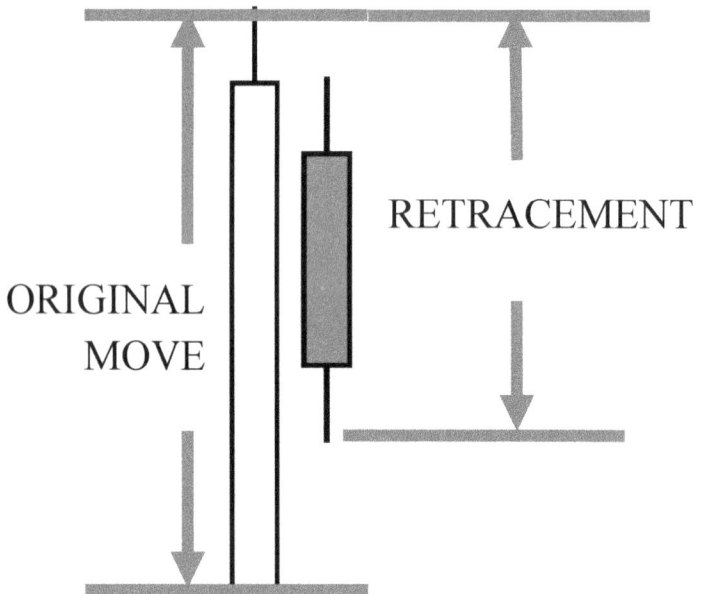

A movement does not have to retrace. Any move has a chance to continue. The weaker the retracement, the stronger the original move.

Triggers are for traders and bears...

You need an objective line - in the case of the bull flag pattern, it's the previous period's high - to *trigger* an entrance. Leave nothing to chance. It's hard enough to suppress your emotions of fear and greed. You need a simple unbiased system. Don't let any of the execution scare you. If you feel uncertain, anxious, or fearful, this is no way to trade. Look back to *Self Control*.

Between the hammer candle, the kicker combo, the flat top breakout, and the bull flag pattern, you are now armed with four weapons to increase your edge significantly. These are market-tested. Now, you need to merge the ideas with your _Style_ and begin to market-test your own strategy.

Trends are your friends...

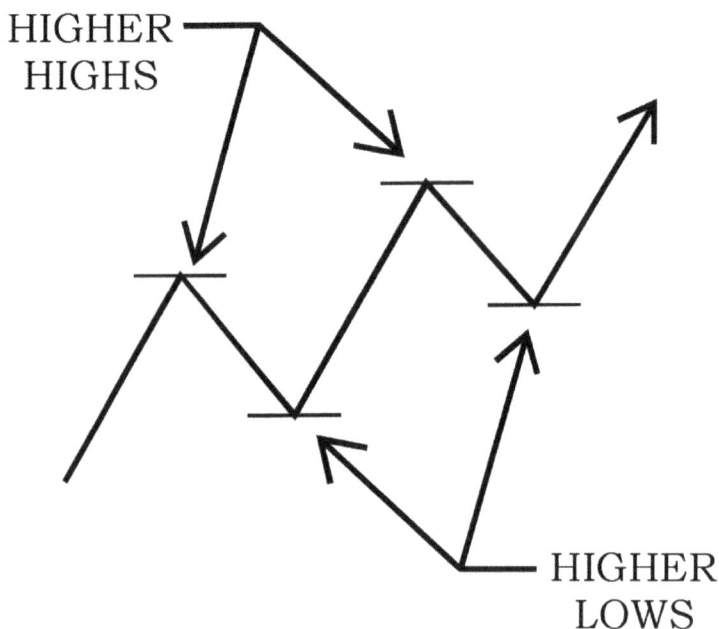

HIGHER HIGHS

HIGHER LOWS

Starting from left to right, the price action runs higher, then there is a "bull pullback" to a low. Don't confuse the bull pullback with a trend reversal. What makes the uptrend is the higher lows and the higher highs.

Even downtrends can be friends...

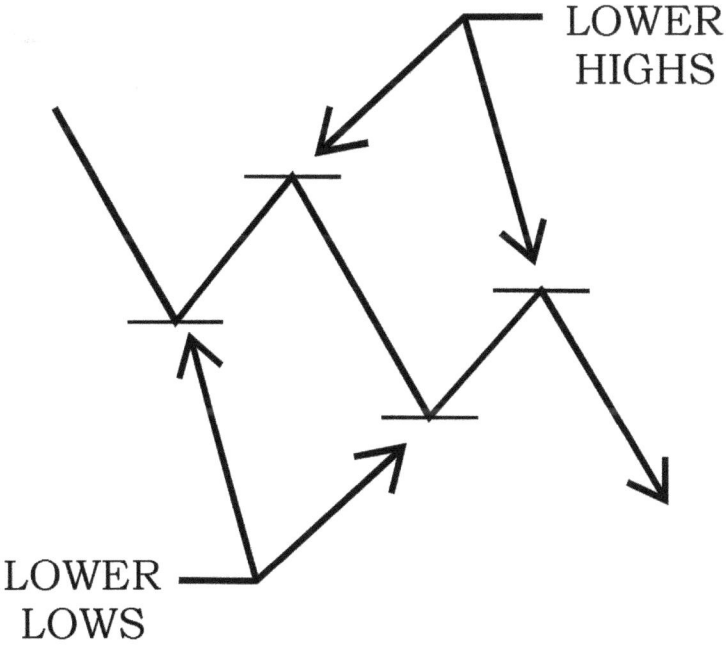

LOWER
HIGHS

LOWER
LOWS

Starting from left to right, the price action falls, then there is a "bear rally" to a high. Don't confuse the bear rally with a trend reversal. What makes the downtrend is the lower lows and the lower highs.

Trends can continue for much longer than expected. There are also seasonal trends to be aware of, which help you to know when to put away your weapons. These seasonal trends aren't really increasing your edge because they are situational. You wouldn't buy right before Black Friday; you would wait for the opportune moment.

It's just that time of **Season**...

The January effect...

Hot stocks go cold in January. Traders *and* investors wait until January to sell their big gainers. They wait until the new year so they don't have to pay taxes on their capital gains until the next year. When you think of January, think the trends are over.

JMT
   ⊕ *Trends are your friends, and friends get tired in January*

The end-of-quarter trend (March, June, September, December)...

Mutual funds are required to report their top holdings on a quarterly basis. When nearing the end of a quarter, you may see selling of losers and buying of winners. This is known as "window dressing." The funds are painting a picture of success by *temporarily* switching positions at quarter's end, which effectively entices buyers.

Election year trends...

The third year of an election cycle is the best year for the overall market, historically speaking. Again, this is not a reason to make a trade, but it could be a reason to avoid one. These seasonal trends and general price trends should be used in confluence with tells and common sense to heighten confidence levels.

Learn the market **tells**...

Just as good card players use tells to get an edge, you can learn market tells to increase your edge moving forward. You don't want to use any one tell as the reason to enter or exit your positions. Use a confluence of all the market tells to increase your certainty. Sticking with positions you have high confidence in will increase performance and your probability of success.

There is always reversion back to the mean. The mean price, or average price, is always changing. Track the period moving averages - like the nine, twenty, fifty or even two hundred period averages - to have a point of reference for future price movement.

The MACD, moving average convergence divergence, is the most common of momentum tells. This tell tracks the momentum of price movement by relating two moving averages: a longer-term price moving average vs. a shorter-term moving average.

I use the MACD in a certain way; others may use it or teach it to you differently, depending on their style. There is no right or wrong way, however you may find one way works better for you.

When the MACD line crosses above the signal line *when the cross occurs above the zero line*, it's a bullish indication. When the MACD crosses below the signal line *when the cross occurs below the zero line,* it's a bearish indication. See figures.

MACD line crossing below Signal line.

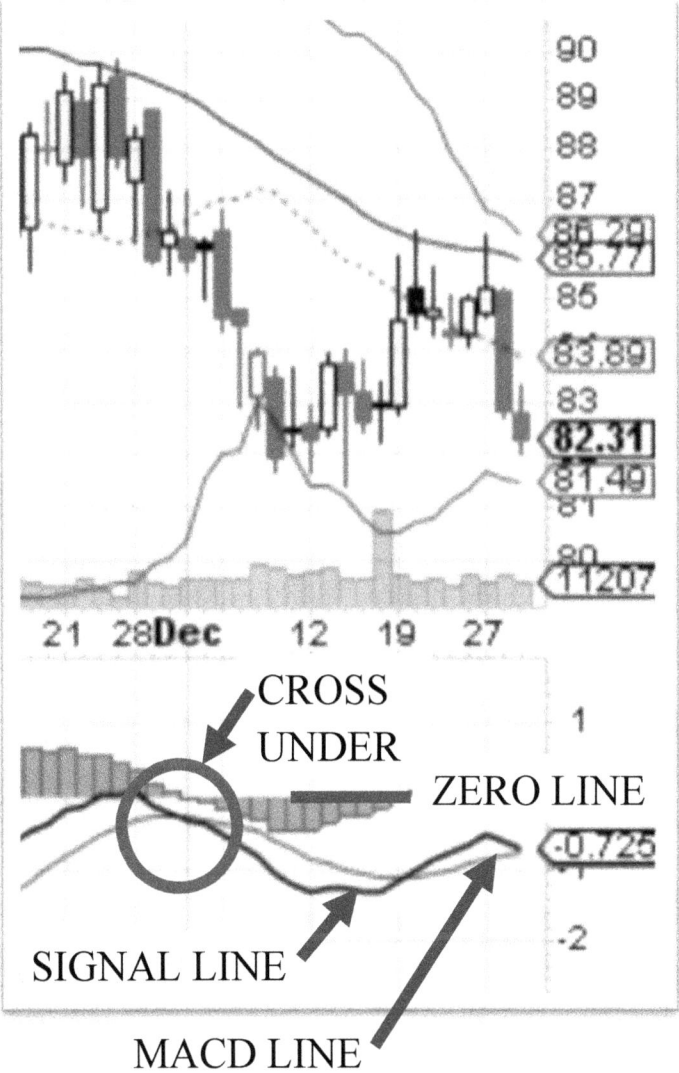

Chart Courtesy of ©Stockcharts.com

MACD line crossing above Signal line.

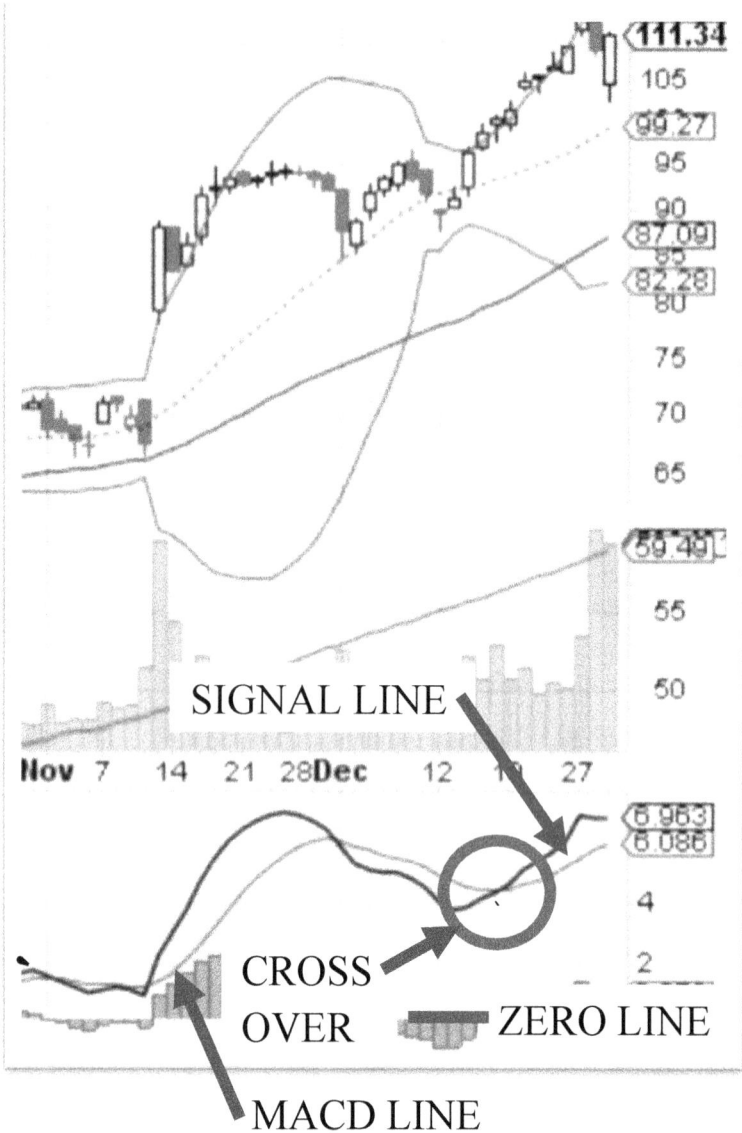

SIGNAL LINE

CROSS OVER

ZERO LINE

MACD LINE

Chart Courtesy of ©Stockcharts.com

The next tell is the Relative Strength Index (RSI).

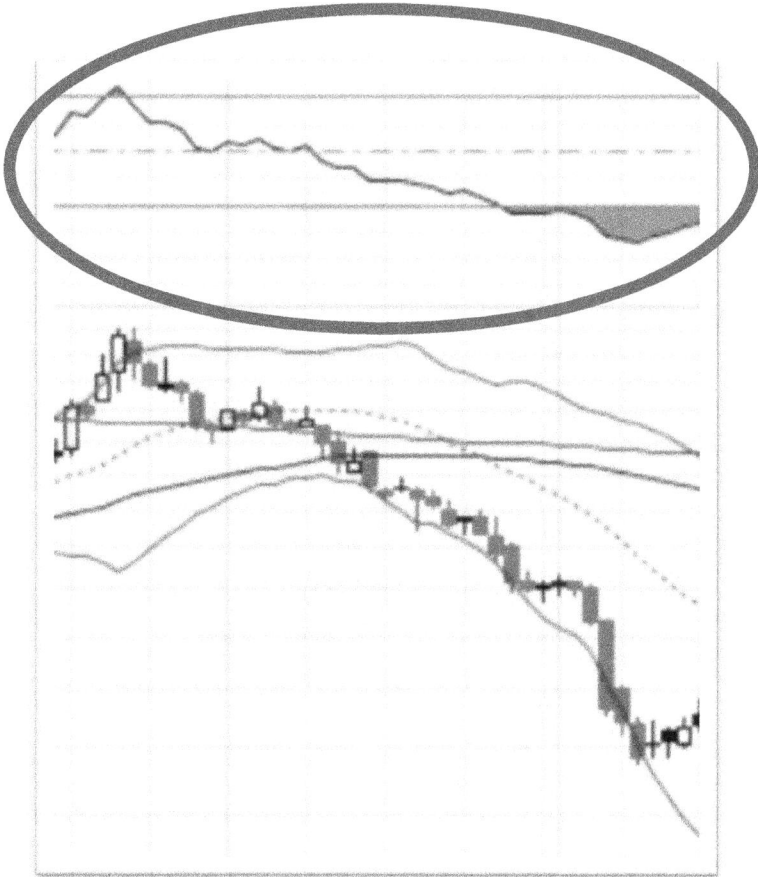

Chart Courtesy of ©Stockcharts.com

The Relative Strength Index is shown atop stockcharts.com as a default feature.

Relative Strength Index

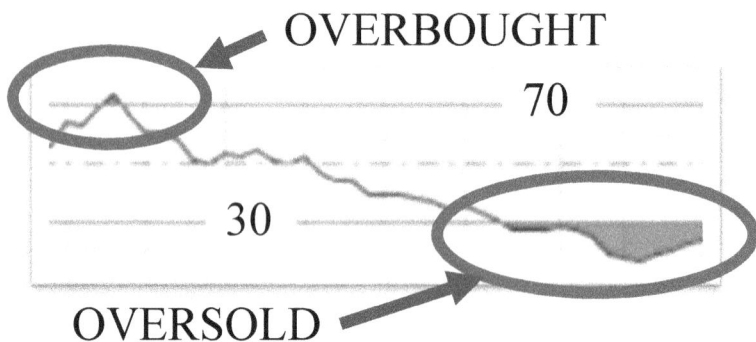

This is another momentum oscillator. Traditional interpretation says above the 70 level (top line) represents overbought territory, and below the 30 level (bottom line) represents oversold. When this oscillator reaches its upper limits, it's a sign that the price of the asset may be becoming overvalued. When this oscillator reaches its lower limits, it's a sign that the price of the asset may be becoming undervalued.

One tell should never be used solely, because a single tell is not very reliable. You want to use them in confluence with your other _Intel_. Examine all information available to you to make the most educated decision in the moment, for your situation.

Finally, the Bollinger Bands dictate approximately 89% of the trading range. Approximately eleven percent of the time, the close price falls outside the probable range as dictated by the upper and lower band. The following figure shows two consecutive days with the close price outside the daily Bollinger Bands.

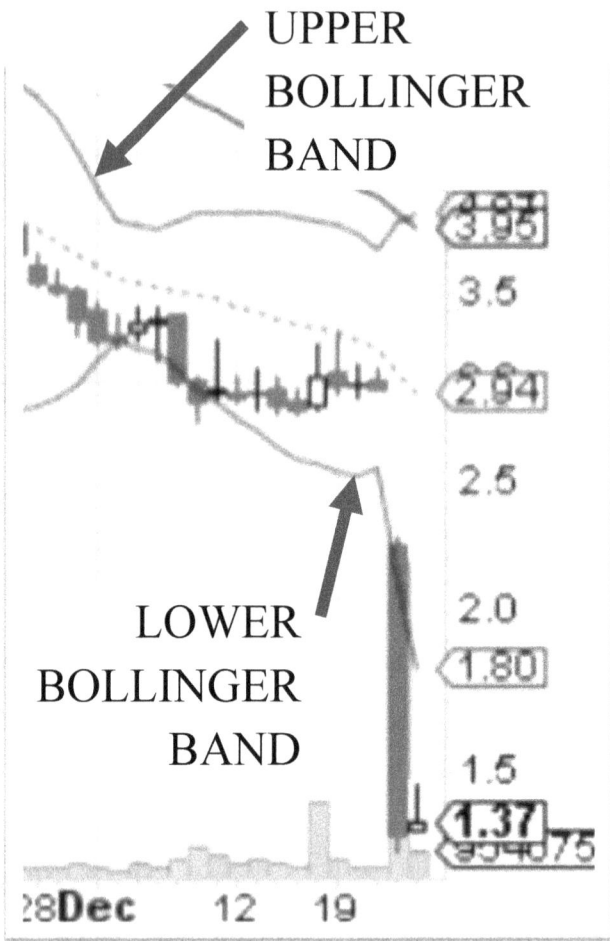

UPPER BOLLINGER BAND

LOWER BOLLINGER BAND

Chart Courtesy of ©Stockcharts.com

When the current price is well below or well above the Bollinger Band range, the price tends to revert back toward the range.

Secret of the Industry...

In 2015, I teamed up with a proprietary trading firm in the industry. I naturally gravitated to a company that focused on education more than anything.

What attracted me was this company's track-record: profit from trade alerts was 100% in 2008, and 50% in 09' and 10'.

If you're interested in teaming up with like-minded traders, just reach out to me and title your email "Prop trading."

Top Down

MARKET

SECTOR

STOCK

Bottom Up

If I am looking to open a longer-term position in the market, I use the top down approach. This approach looks at the overall market movement first, then the sector, and then the individual stock.

The broad market makes up 50% of the movement of a company, strictly based on statistics.

PRICE ACTION BASIS

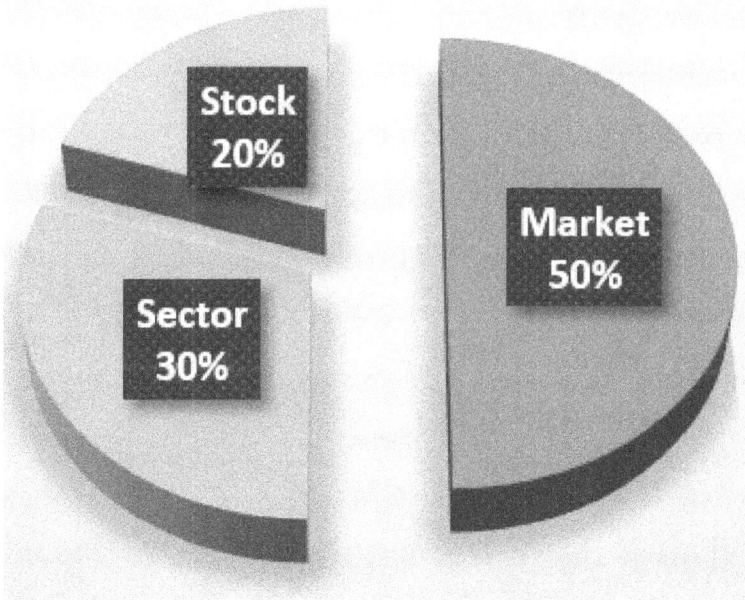

Stock 20%

Market 50%

Sector 30%

When a trade is made in today's world, there is a 30% chance it was made based solely on the performance of a sector. Realizing this may help explain certain movements in the market.

Here are the sector exchange-traded funds, and their respective ticker symbols. These reflect how each sector is performing:

Utilities sector (XLU)
Telecom (IYZ)
Real estate (IYR)
Industrials (XLI)
Healthcare (XLV)
Financials (XLF)
Consumer (IYC)
Technology (XLK)
Materials (XLB)
Energy (XLE)

Trust your *Intel.*

CHAPTER IV

SELF CONFIDENCE

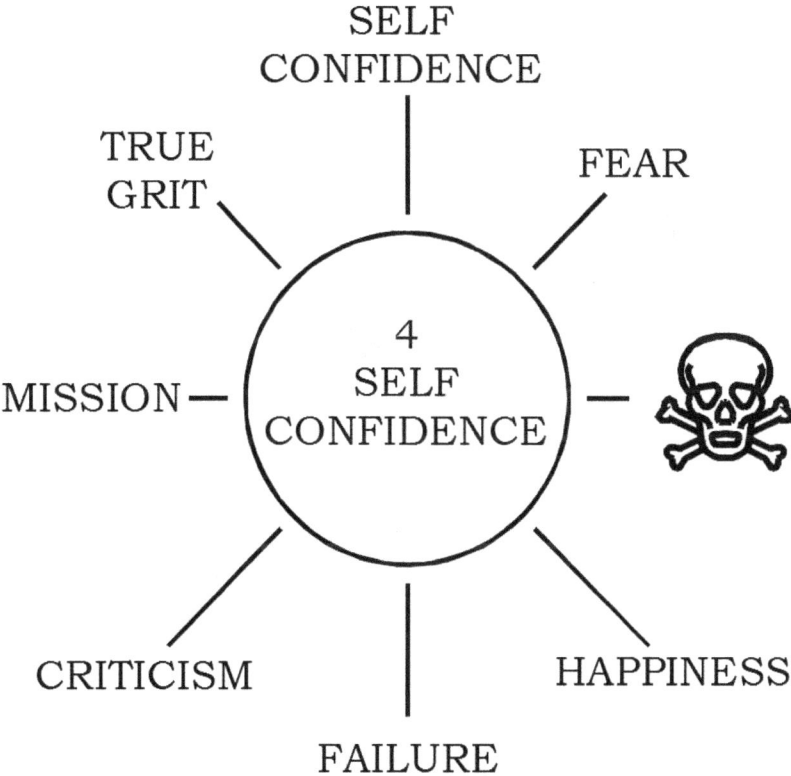

Many people expect to be successful blindly mirroring a professional's portfolio. There is something to that; it's just not the *right* thing. I was guilty of this in the beginning. I thought if I held the same positions as the pros, I would get the same returns. I lacked **Self Confidence**. I didn't have the right *Intel* either.

Simply mirroring a pro's positions is a flawed approach on many levels. First, to mirror any exact position entry and exit, you need to constantly follow the source, at least during market hours. Second, if you are putting full trust in one source for entries and exits, this shows you don't have *faith* in your own judgement. You ultimately need faith in your own plan to be able to attain peace of mind while carrying out your desire.

Self confidence increases with knowledge and the quality of your _Intel_. The most powerful weapon in your arsenal, to fight those trying to strip you of your poise, is your mind. Just like positive thoughts can bring good health, negative thoughts can bring disease. Ignore all negativity as if it were a plague.

If _it_ is constantly on your mind, the likelihood of _it_ happening sky-rockets over time. Good, bad, or ugly, your dominating thoughts have a way of surfacing in your reality. Surprise!

JMT

⊕ _You're at the pinnacle of your health_

The only thing to **fear** is *fear* itself...

Fear neglects all truths that may lift you up. It overcomes the average Service Member; however, it never disrupts the master. Fear is nothing more than a state of mind. Your state of mind is subject to control and direction.

Fear of public speaking tops the list of greatest fears. The next time you're at a funeral, consider that the person reading the eulogy may prefer the casket.

> "Death smiles at us all; all you can do is smile back."
> ~ *Marcus Aurelius*

Why do you fear financial instability? Financial difficulties threaten our survival, the soul of our existence. The one thing we are all *forced* to do is to survive. So how do you trump the fear of poverty? The idea is to thrive. Stimulate your mind to *react positively* to any situation and always maintain the belief you are going to do your absolute best with where you are and what you have.

There are two ways to think. You can think, "*I can't* get *it*," in which case you never will. The alternative is to think, "*How can I* get *it*?" This seemingly insignificant difference is extremely powerful. The curse of the poverty-stricken mindset induces questions of identity, and this *idea* of low self-worth. There are only a few things worse.

In the movie *It's a Wonderful Life*, the main character George Bailey, played by the late, great Jimmy

Stewart, was told by the richest man in town that he is worth more dead than alive. This drove George to the brink of suicide. George was a victim of his circumstances, as we all are. Mr. Potter, that rich man, who so closely resembled Ebenezer Scrooge, couldn't see the beauty of George Bailey's business strategy to promote home-grown homes, and, in a moment of weakness, neither could George.

It took weathering the storm, and the help of an angel named Clarence, for George to come to his senses and remember he truly did have a wonderful life.

> "Live everyday like it's your last, and one day you'll be right."
> ~ *Steve Jobs*

Images of fire and brimstone may circle your mind when faced with thoughts of death. The truth is, no one on God's green earth knows if a heaven or a hell exists.

Fear of **death** is a fear of the unknown. The only known for all of us is that death is unavoidable. When you think of death as a necessary part of life, it doesn't seem quite so bad. Better to have lived and lost, then not lived at all.

Is **happiness** relative?

To answer the question "Is happiness relative?", a group of researchers from Northwestern and the University of Massachusetts, compared a group of lottery winners with a group accident victims.

It turned out that the lottery winners were not happier than the accident victims when all was said and done. In fact, the lottery winners took significantly less pleasure from a series of regular, daily activities.

For a measure of everyday pleasure, respondents were asked to rate how pleasant they found each of these seven activities or events: talking with a friend, watching television, eating break-

fast, hearing a funny joke, getting a compliment, reading a magazine, and buying clothes... All ratings were made on 6-point scales ranging from 0 for "not at all" to 5 for "very much." [P]

The control group's 'mundane pleasure' mean (average) rating was 3.82, while the average accident victim's ratings were 3.48. The lottery winners had the lowest rating of 3.33.

When you receive something for nothing, you may find there is no appreciation for it because it wasn't earned. Real happiness is achieved by working for *it*. Fixate on creating wealth, not money.

[P] Journal of Personality and Social Psychology 1978, Vol. 36, No. 8, 917-927, Phillip Brickman, Dan Coates, and Ronnie Janoff-Bulman, *Lottery Winners and Accident Victims: Is Happiness Relative?*

So where can you learn the most valuable wealth creating lessons? One way to learn is by following those who do it well.

Every **failure** carries with it the seed of an equivalent benefit. Search deep into the possible benefits of your failures. Don't dwell on the failure, dwell on the benefits.

It's easy to **criticize**...

Most of the time, it's better to keep your mouth shut and your thoughts just where they are. Critics can be harsh and detrimental to your journey. If you feel the need to criticize, do it in private. It's hard to recover from hurting a friend's pride. When you are criticized, focus on criticism that has some sort of truth, while dismissing the purely negative chatter. Use the critics to point out your biggest flaws. Finding your greatest flaw will lead you to wealth twice as fast.

JMT
   ⊕ *You only give public praise*

Study every single decision in your life, but don't dwell on a single one. Make a decision and stick with it; however, as soon as you realize you're wrong, correct yourself immediately.

In David Ramsey's blog, he notes 6% of the wealthy say what's on their mind vs. 69% of the poor.[R]

[R] http://www.daveramsey.com/blog/20-things-the-rich-do-every-day

JMT

⊕ *You don't say what's on your mind unless it will help*

Wealthy people are thinking the same thing as you and me; they are not saying it aloud because it doesn't help. Saying what's on your mind can distract you from working the problem. If you choose words carefully, you may be able to change the tune of the whole situation for the better.

Our unfiltered thoughts can be hurtful and detrimental to another Service Member's growth. Often, we don't realize our impact on someone else's world until it's too late. There are two things you can't get back: words after they are spoken and time after it's wasted. I'll get back to wasted time in *Organization*.

Use **facts** as the basis for your decisions...

Facts are only as good as their sources. Every fact must be put into perspective by considering both the position of the speaker and the soundness of his or her reasoning. Today, mis-information is floating around *more than ever before.*

Make decisions promptly and base your decisions on quality facts from respected sources. Don't change your mind unless necessary. If no new facts are presented, there is no need to re-examine your decision. One trait among successful people is decisiveness. Indecision is just as crippling as procrastination.

True grit...

You aren't going to be successful right away. Plan to fail, especially at first. There is a very high failure rate -94%- for *beginners* in the market. Don't give up after the first few thousand failures. True grit is sticking to your guns until you gain confidence in your style and mastery of your positions.

There is nothing that boosts confidence more than a simulated market or real life role playing. Once you find a good market measure, you can begin to test your strategy. If you stick with *it* consistently, and surround yourself with the most successful that are doing *it*, it's only a matter of time before your true grit will prevail.

CHAPTER V
TEAM

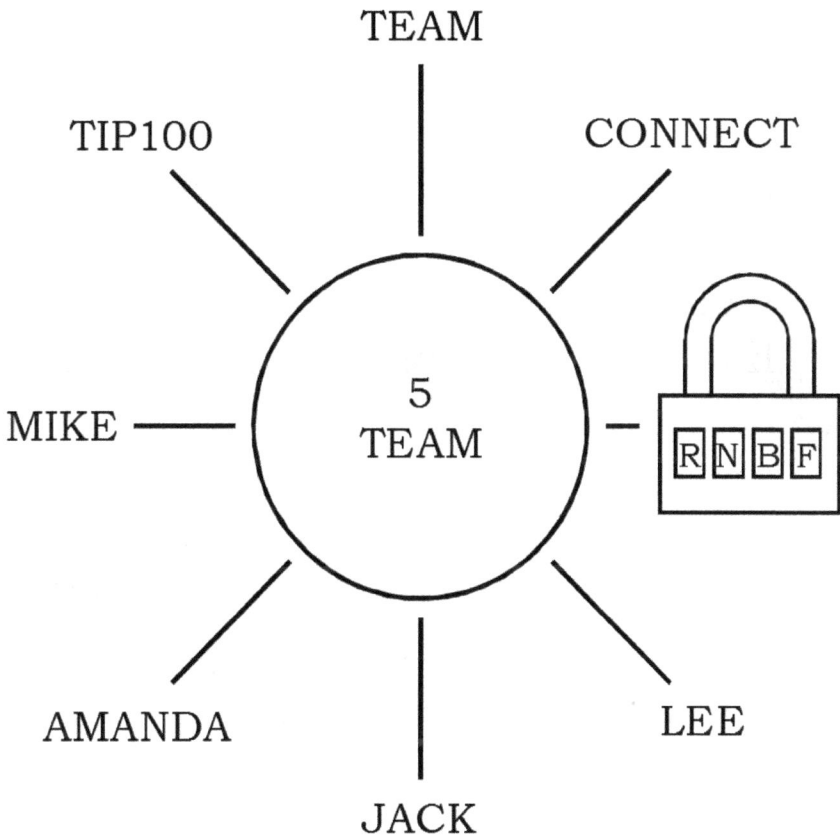

Team math…

1 Mind + 1 Mind = 2 Minds

JMT
  ⊕ *You know what you want, now double your efforts*

Often, we expect the leader to discover the breakthrough that leads to the game-changing moment for a team. In reality, however, the breakthrough often comes from a regular team member, not the leader. The leader needs a bird's eye view of operations, and therefore is not usually grinding to find the major problem pass-through, and shouldn't be. As a leader, you have more important problems to think about.

In the 1980's, Charlie Wilson, a seemingly ordinary Congressman from Texas, was *the* catalyst that sparked the Russian exit from Afghanistan during the Cold War. Some argue Charlie singlehandedly changed the world.

In the movie, Charlie Wilson's War, based on the true story, one of Charlie's first actions was to double the budget of the Afghan desk from five million to ten million. As the movie depicts well, many powerful people were highly critical of this action. The bump from five to ten million seemed so insignificant against a much greater Russian Army. A case where great desire met great opposition.

It's important to remember, if Charlie had done nothing, he would have not been criticized at all. Doubling the money was the first logical step in Charlie's strategy to raise attention to the problem at hand. Although many were quick to criticize, no one was doing anything about the problem except for Charlie.

As harsh as it may be, welcome the criticism with open arms and do not let it disrupt your mission.

Special Forces are invaluable. Special Forces are always sent in teams. When does the government ever send *one* Navy SEAL anywhere? Everyone knows SEAL team six from "Zero Dark Thirty". There are eight SEAL teams. Each SEAL team has six platoons. SEAL team members are a rare breed. You can't train just anyone in the skills required for this position.

Going on a mission with a platoon increases the odds of everyone's success. A team working together in unison, toward a common goal, has a much better chance of accomplishing the mission.

When you look at Special Forces teams, certain skills are required of every member. For example, all Navy SEALs are required to be skilled in diving, parachuting *and* demolition. Whatever your chosen field, certain basic skills are required to compete.

Connect with Mentors...

Each good mentor increases your chance of success by 2%. Surround yourself with the most responsive, best-in-class support you can find. Not just anyone, you need superstars. Superstars can't help but teach you their most valuable secrets. A great team can be a huge confidence builder. Training in a great team can separate you entirely from all others.

The beauty of business...

If you are trying to make a profit in any market, there are several advantages to forming an entity to represent the *business* you are conducting. This *business* can make millions over the course of a few years starting with little to nothing. The only prerequisite for starting a business is the honest effort to make a profit.

You can be a one-man or a one-woman army. You don't have to have a team. You don't have to start a business. However, this is a step-by-step guide on *creating wealth*, so I don't want to gloss over important details. The odds of success increase significantly with a team of mentors and a business entity.

So, why does it make sense to start a business to secure your wealth? It's less risky and there are hidden benefits.

How is it less risky? It is separate from you and protected by laws just like you. When you create a business, the business has its own insurance and its own assets. The business can sue or be sued. If you own a business, and it's set up correctly, you are personally protected against claims related to business operations.

What are the benefits to starting a business? Most people have a car, a phone, an internet connection, and a space that they use to operate their business. These expenses *may be* tax deductible assuming they relate to your business *and you actually have one.* To start a business, you only need a few things and I'll help you get them.

A business is no more than an *idea*. You don't need any money to start thinking of an idea! Come up with a unique name for your business. You'll need to determine the state in which you want to register your legal business entity. Your legal entity will be subject to business laws in the state it is registered.

Most of the time it makes sense to register in the state in which you operate. Requirements vary by state; however, the process usually involves filling out a form or two and paying a small fee.

A lawyer can walk you through the process for a tax-deductible fee, or you can search for the information online yourself, as it pertains to your state. If you think you can profit in any market, it may make sense to start a business. If you aren't familiar with appropriate record keeping for your industry, hire an accountant.

Why do you need a business *team*? It's much easier with one. Draw from your best sources of <u>Intel</u> and trust your sources. Trust increases speed and lowers cost. Find someone who is doing it better than anyone else, and someone you trust. Often, these superstars are begging to give away their knowledge for free. If you need to pay mentors, pay the mentors. It's worth it.

Find the best talent the market has to offer and strategically build your team. When you find your team, all your mirrors will turn into windows.

It's not *what* you know, it's *who* you know. This cliché used to aggravate me, and it still does a little, mainly because knowing *this* doesn't help *in the moment*. After reading this chapter, hopefully you will get some ideas as to who you might need on your team. I will introduce you to a few good mentors who helped me to get my message out. Don't be afraid to reach out to me or them. You never know where it will take you.

Separation dulls relationships and breaks bonds. There is a way however, to stay connected at all times. This is achieved by believing, feeling, and acting like you are very much connected. I'll get to more on this in *Personal Courage*. The more connected you are to everyone, the more you will be able to work together in a spirit of harmony toward a common goal.

Rapport, Needs, Benefits, Follow-up...

This is the secret combination to unlock your team. Rapport is the first step. Show others that you care. Be interested in them, or they won't be interested in you. Show them benefits of knowing you, and show them you're not going away, ever.

Don't try to unlock a relationship unless you can see mutual benefits in the future. Only go after superstars that can take you to the next level.

Lee...

I was first introduced to Lee through the Corps of Engineers after joining their Leadership Development Program. The first year, one of the assigned books was "Creating Magic" by Lee Cockerell.

Lee has an impressive resume. He managed over 40,000 Cast Members, and 5,000 managers while serving as the Vice President of Operations of one of the largest companies in the world.

Lee is a superstar. When I emailed Lee for the first time on a Sunday night, he responded in twenty minutes. I will never forget that. Lee didn't know me. He probably gets hundreds, if not thousands of emails a day. That day, I knew I had found a true superstar.

I like to think Lee could *sense the potential in me.* Lee recommended what became one of my greatest sources of knowledge. I share this source in *Personal Courage*.

Keep in mind, my relationship with Lee started with me joining a program at work - a program that required me to do more work for the same amount of money.

Don't know **Jack**?

Through the source that Lee provided, and a virtual intermediary, I was introduced to Jack Nadel, an international entrepreneur who profited every year for nearly seven decades.

Jack was released from active duty in WWII, having survived 27 intense and increasingly more dangerous combat missions in a B-29 bomber over Japan. He founded, acquired, and operated more than a dozen companies, creating thousands of jobs and millions in profits. Action-packed and full of useful advice, Jack's book, *The Evolution of an Entrepreneur,* keeps the reader on edge while delivering practical ways to create wealth by finding needs and filling them. That's what *business* is all about.

One lesson I learned from his book was to not let my ego get in the way of a profitable business.

Jack was presented with a Watch Band Calendar, a product from a friend. He really didn't like the product but, because of his relationship with the seller, he ultimately decided to send it to his sales team. Twenty-two million Watch Band Calendars later, he learned to love the amazing product!

Even if you don't like a product or service, keep an open mind: it may not be worthless.

Amanda...

I connected with Amanda Holmes on LinkedIn after reading her father's book, *The Ultimate Sales Machine*. She is CEO of Chet Holmes International, a business that generates hundreds of millions in revenue each year.

Amanda and her team helped me to get my work researched by the largest college district in the country. We are now working together, with the help of a university sponsorship, to offer a free online workshop for Military and Veterans detailing how to achieve 30% returns *or more* on your savings.

After connecting with Amanda, I had the privilege of spending hours watching recorded trainings of Chet Holmes himself, as he imparted his wisdom to an audience of hundreds of high level executives from all around the country.

After those trainings, I became convinced the late great Chet Holmes was truly a master. Chet got 60 of the Fortune 500 companies to buy his services *by cold calling* the CEO's. Chet worked directly for Charlie Munger, close partner of Warren Buffet. Charlie put Chet in charge of nine divisions of a company. Chet doubled sales of many divisions for several years consecutively.

Amanda and her team, with the help of Dr. Todd Eller, are helping to build my message to my audience.

Mike, Captain of *the best damn ship in the Navy...*

I was introduced to Mike in the exact same way I was introduced to Lee. I read his book in my Leadership Development Program. So, although I was introduced to Jack and Amanda through Lee Cockerell's ONE source, I was still gaining more connections through all possible channels.

Captain D. Michael Abrashoff writes a great story in his book *It's Your Ship* about how he unified the USS *Benfold*. As Captain, he wanted to change the ineffective 'diversity training' the Navy had in place on the ship, because it wasn't working. He did something unheard of... He *cancelled* the diversity training altogether, for which he could have been fired.

In place of the diversity training, he substituted what he called 'unity training.' The new program was his own creation. The program was focused on helping Service Members to discover each other's likenesses and common goals, instead of focusing on each other's differences. Mike describes 'unity training' as maximizing uniqueness and channeling focus toward common group goals.

After reading *It's Your Ship*, you'll see how the *Benfold* got its reputation as "the best damn ship in the Navy." So, why do I bring up *this* story from Mike's book? The best course of action for you is not in any book, and you won't find any cookie cutter one-size-fits-all solution to any of the challenges that you will face on your journey.

Everything in life is situational. For Mike, making progress meant that he had to throw out the institutionalized training completely, *something which could have cost him his job*, to create something new to solve his specific problem, which was a dysfunctional ship. That was the out-of-the-box solution, and the story captures nicely the attributes of good leadership that made such a move both possible and effective.

TIP100...

Of course I had to put *myself* on your team! TIP100 is The Inflection Point Inc.'s own creation designed to be "your *best* source for market trends," and offers continued support for your wealth creation journey. The videos I create are meant to teach market patterns, as shown in the _Intel_ Chapter. I also highlight the differences in _Style_ when moving from a shorter timeframe to a longer one.

I offer one trade highlight, usually based on the stock's 15-minute chart, as a potential trade for the upcoming week. I highlight just one trade to simplify the process. I also offer trade templates free of charge if you are a Service Member or Veteran and for those who have purchased this book. The trade template offers flawless executing by automating your exit, something which traders seem to struggle with the most.

I have 100% confidence anyone can take this template and the weekly video, and earn over 30% every year. The exact patterns are shown with the entrances and exits noted on the chart.

Although I'm the only one shooting the videos as of now, I do have a large team of financial advisors, analysts, managers, engineers, editors, and other traders that I look to for input on the videos. Depending on the weekly situation, I may call on different sources because the skills each has is very specialized.

Check me out on LinkedIn, and you'll see some of my connections. Connect on Facebook and you'll find even more. Have a specific problem? Let me put you in contact with someone from my team who I know will be able to help you to solve it.

The *mastermind principle* is a principle that states when two or more minds come together, they form a greater mind, known as the mastermind. The mastermind doesn't exist without at least two minds, in harmony, focused on

ONE common goal. When multiple minds act in a spirit of harmony, any goal becomes attainable.

Introductions are everything. If you want me to introduce you to anyone on the team, just ask! My email address is given at the end of the book. I look forward to hearing from you!

CHAPTER VI

ORGANIZATION

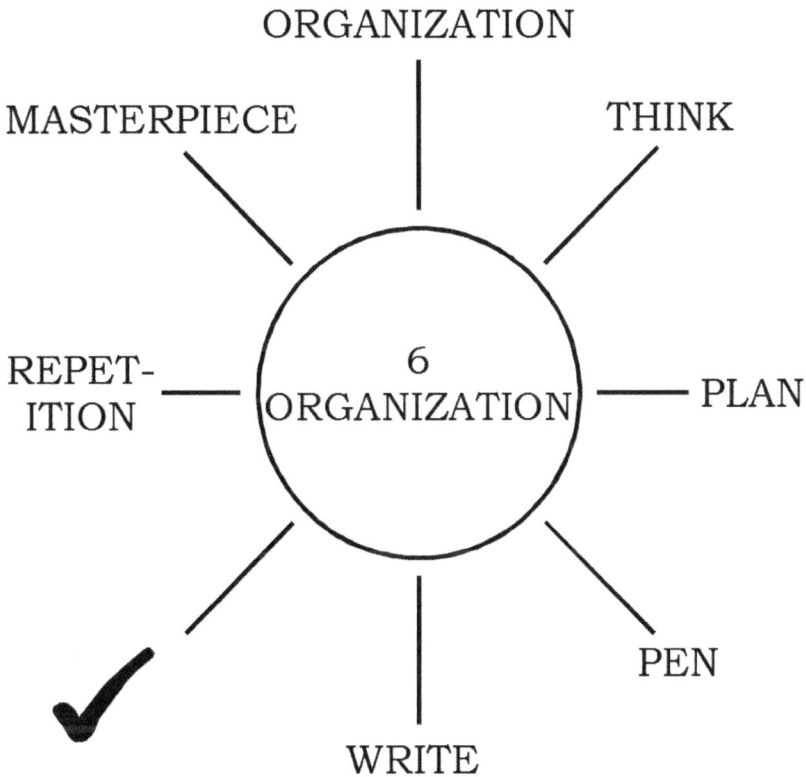

Gain power with **Organization**...

It's the little details in life that define you, not the big ones. Train yourself to observe every single little action you make. Concentrate on making just one change every day for the better in your daily routine. Even one tiny adjustment can have massive implications over the course of your life.

Think...

When you pick something up, take care of it right away; if you can't take care of it right away, don't pick it up.

JMT
⊕ *Touch it once*

It's easy to get off track from what needs your attention right now.

Have one time of the day when you concentrate on planning. The strategist beats the tactician every time. You need extreme concentration to the point of meditation. It's easy to get sidetracked starting something that is not on your critical path.

Doing multiple things at once doesn't help either. Multitasking is proven to hurt performance and it can kill you.

Other things will naturally come up. Stick with your assigned tasks as if you were taking orders from the President and when there is an office fire or rocket alarm, you'll be better prepared for the emergency.

Here is a good example of a process to use:

1. Write out your most important things to do in any order.

2. Pick six of the most important you can do TODAY.

3. Rank and assign durations to those six tasks.

4. Match each of the durations to a specific time slot in your day, ensuring you will complete your #1 task first.

Once the slots are assigned, stick with them no matter what.

RECAP

1. Make a To Do list everyday
   (15 min)

2. Pick six tasks to do today
   (15 min)

3. Assign a duration and priority
   to each task adding up to no
   more than eight hours
   (15 min)

4. Assign a time slot for the first
   six activities with the most
   important task in the first slot
   (15 min)

5. Do the first task first

The only way to ensure
accomplishing 90% of that which
you are capable, is to plan your
day and guard the timeslots as if

they are the President and you are the Secret Service.

Expect success; **plan** for failure...

Why do you need a pocket-sized planner that goes out two years? When I started, I only got one because that is what a few billionaires told me to do. After the first year, I noticed I could look back and see the repeat events: birthdays, friends' parties, vacations, anniversaries, and other annual events. The planner is a tool to help you become a strategist.

Also, a small notebook and a record book to record transactions are very helpful as well. Only one of each. It's important to know your work calendar at home and vice versa. You need ONE. I expect one out of one hundred readers will carry one of these three items. Having these three things can set you apart as a superstar.

The **pen** is mightier than the phone...

Taking notes on your phone may be your style, and it may work. In my experience, people perceive me differently if I am taking notes on my phone vs. taking notes with a pen in my notebook. I carry a pen and planner everywhere I go. Yes, I get made fun of constantly. It hurts the most when the hecklers are little kids, because this simple secret is still not being taught in schools. *Almost everyone* asks me why I don't use my phone. Perception is everything; however, that is not the only reason. I've lost good ideas with phone distractions. One day, a great idea flashed into my mind, and I took my phone out to put the idea in my notes.

When I looked at my phone I saw my missed calls first, then texts, and before I knew it I was checking emails, Facebook, Twitter, Snapchat... the idea got cold. To this day, I don't remember what I was thinking. Don't let your ideas get cold. Phones are great tools at scheduled times. However, if you don't control the exact times you are on your phone, your phone will control you.

With direction from Andrew Carnegie, the richest man in the

world at one point, Napoleon Hill advises writing down your one major desire in life in the beginning of your planner, i.e. "grow bank account to one million". Then, write what you are prepared to give in order to attain this one major desire, i.e. "one hour every market day". Repeat these to yourself twice daily, once when you wake up and once before you retire.

As you read and repeat, see, believe, and feel yourself already in possession of your desire.

Write it down or risk never attaining it...

The following is a story told about students graduating from an Ivy League school. When the students were asked about their goals, results were reported as follows...

3% had written goals.

14% had goals, however they were not written.

86% had no goals.

It was later discovered that on average, the students with goals made three times more money than the students without goals.

Those students with written goals went on to earn ten times more than those without written goals.

Even though it's a story, the message is still powerful and real.

JMT

⊕ *You know what you need to do*

Readiness includes being prepared with certain items all the time. You never know when some great information or opportunity might come your way.

"Success is where preparation meets opportunity." –*Oprah Winfrey*

Now, you'll know to be ready for it. Readiness also includes your mindset. Think about how your attitude affects everything about your situation.

One of the greatest threats to any business is the closed-mindedness of its employees: closed toward others, closed toward the outside world, and closed toward *ideas*. Take all suggestions seriously, as one may save your life.

✓

Checklists,Checklists,Checklists...

Checklists can be used to improve every aspect of your life. Use them when trading in your market.

Atul Gawande is famous for his research on the subject of checklists. The effectiveness of using checklists is supported by many situations examined in his book *Checklist Manifesto*.

Dr. Gawande relates one story about the Army testing its new Model 299 plane. During a test run, the plane stalled and crashed in a fiery explosion. It was determined that the crash was a result of "pilot error." This aircraft was much more complex than previous aircraft, and it was thought that perhaps the pilot was not able to keep track of all steps necessary to keep the plane in the air.

The pilot needed to attend to the four engines, a retractable landing gear, new wing flaps, electric trim tabs needed adjustment to maintain control at different airspeeds, and constant-speed propellers whose pitch had to be regulated with hydraulic controls, among other features.

In trying to solve the problem of how to overcome the difficulty created by the complexity of this new aircraft, several things were considered. Could additional training prevent pilot error? Major Hill, who had been the main pilot in the crash, was a highly experienced pilot. Therefore, more training was thrown out as a possible solution. Instead, the Army came up with the idea of assembling a pilot's checklist with a step-by-step procedure for takeoff, flight, landing and taxiing.

With checklist in hand, pilots went on to fly 1.8 million miles without one accident. The Army ultimately ordered almost thirteen thousand of the aircraft, which it dubbed the B-17... the Army gained a decisive air advantage in World War II which enabled its devastating campaign against Nazi Germany.

Dr. Gawande also provides a story of checklists saving lives in hospitals.

(In 2006) *researchers at Johns Hopkins University published the results of a program that was instituted in nearly every intensive care unit in Michigan - a simple five-step checklist designed to prevent certain hospital infections...*

The results were stunning. Within three months of using the checklist, the rate of bloodstream infections fell by two-thirds. The I.C.U.s cut their infection rates from 4 percent to zero. Over 18 months, the program saved more than 1,500 lives and nearly $200 million.[A]

[A]Atul Gawande, *Checklist Manifesto,* 2009

It is very difficult to make progress without organization, and a checklist is a proven method of organizing.

Repetition is the mother of skill...

All skills require repetition to get to the mastery level. It is boring until it's excellent. If you want to become proficient, you need to commit a set amount of time per day or per week to practice. This commitment must be FOREVER. That's why when you pick your vehicle, you need to know it's *the* ONE.

If you spend one hour per day studying your subject, you can be an international expert in seven years. Only a small percentage of us have the discipline to carry out a plan consistently over the course of seven years.

One thing I wanted to do in my life was to be able to juggle a soccer ball 100 times without dropping it. When I was at Rowan University in South Jersey, I tried to juggle with some Rowan soccer players. One guy, Mike Hall, could juggle the soccer ball forever. Seriously, when I asked him how many times he could juggle in a row, he said he could go forever, until he collapsed.

Most of the soccer players in the juggling circle were better than I was, but because we played so often, maybe an hour or two every day, I slowly got better.

They could all pass the ball to themselves very easily with a soft touch. When I was in the group, I started to pay more attention because a severe mis-touch was rather embarrassing and disruptive. It started to occur to me the spin on the ball was a big factor. I needed to adjust my touch to the situation, but I still couldn't do it.

I lacked consistency. After finishing college, I stopped juggling for a few years never having reached 100 touches. Just in the last few months, I picked it up again after I saw a soccer ball in a store. It turns out, it's a lot like riding a bike. I started back up at about 10 to 15 touches at best, with most attempts just two to five touches. I told myself I would get better every day.

After scheduling one hour a day to juggle, it took less than 20 one-hour sessions to break through the teens and make higher highs. When I got to 50, I knew I was close to success.

The very next time, I scheduled a few hours, and told myself I wasn't stopping until 100. In the very last minutes when the sun was setting, I got 100 touches on the soccer ball without it ever touching the ground.

The next time I went out to juggle, the goal was 200 and I got 200 the very next time.

Waste time with the **masterpiece**...

A journey of 10,000 steps starts with ONE step.

The masterpiece signifies genuine mastery, probably best known and most easily recognized in the art world. If you want to create the world's best art, start by following the best-known artist.

An artist talented enough to create a masterpiece has fine-tuned his or her skills through hard work and repetition. When you see the masterpiece, it's easy to forget the thousands of imperfect pieces that paved the way.

Without all previous attempts and failures, the masterpiece would never exist. The masterpiece is significant, because it illustrates control of every single little detail. Just like a masterpiece, your organization must be created one perfect feature at a time.

My mom is a master of organization. It was most likely out of necessity, because of how absent-minded I was growing up. I was told by *almost everyone* I would lose my head if it wasn't attached. Even little tasks, like getting ready on time, were insurmountable challenges to me. I would manage to oversleep or fall in the toilet and make myself late.

My mom would label my belongings with a black permanent marker, which she kept sealed in a freezer bag. This began in elementary school and continued through high school to the point of embarrassment.

It wasn't until I experienced the real world and a number of failures, that I realized that my mom is an organization genius and that being organized is the only way to get more done every day. Organization is a penalty the ambitious must pay. A couple years ago, I was forced to get organized.

One thing I learned from my mom is that if you really want something to fit together like a puzzle, you need to dismantle the entire thing, piece by piece, to examine the size and shape it will take up in your life.

When you carefully examine the size and shape of your belongings, you can begin to put them away or trash them. When my mom cleans, she is notorious for trashing items that someone else might have thought of as useful. To my mom, however, it is only clutter. Clutter causes confusion, hesitation, and indecision. Clear the clutter, envision your big picture, and create your masterpiece one small, seemingly insignificant piece at a time.

There was an episode of the Simpsons in which their house was going up in flames, and Marge is rushing to do the dishes in the sink right before the house explodes. That is my mom.

When my mom leaves the house, you won't find a glass in the sink, a sock on the floor, an unmade bed, *or even* a foot imprint in the dining room. Growing up, my siblings and I weren't allowed to set foot in the dining room. The footprint would show on the perfect streaks of vacuuming. It didn't hit me until a decade later that this seemingly obsessive - compulsive behavior allows everything else to become easier or insignificant.

Even when I experienced it every day, I didn't get it. I would question every aspect of the cleanliness, to the point of getting extremely angry about my things getting misplaced or trashed. I suppose it is a natural reaction of self-expression to lash out and want to disobey parental guidance.

JMT

⊕ *You trust those with more experience*

It wasn't until I had long moved out, that I began to understand the subtle tricks my mom used to make everything else easier. Eventually, I realized the value of organization and worked to incorporate more organization into my life.

Organization, like most things, is incremental. Improve just one thing a day, and your life will start to fall into place like dominoes. If you make organization a continuous goal, it will make all the difference.

Ask yourself, "What can I do today, right now, that by doing so, everything else becomes easier or irrelevant?" It's simple, yet almost never at the forefront of your thoughts. It forces you to take a step back, and look at your big picture.

Now, my mom never forced me to have a planner. I can picture her saying "Oh God, David" in response to me completely forgetting about (insert important event here).

She probably never forced it on me because she thought it would never take, and I'm not going to lie, it probably wouldn't have. After all, she couldn't even get me to put my dirty socks directly in the hamper.

After 27 years, I finally started to listen to my mom instead of letting her words pass through my brain like a sieve. I remember going away for work not too long ago and telling her I forgot something. She asked if I had written it on my *packing list*.

I didn't have a packing list then, but I do now. I still forget things. When I realize, I add those specific items to the list so I never forget the same thing twice. Thanks Mom!

There is time everywhere in your schedule, you just need to find it. For me, I traced the items I carry every day on white paper and taped those outlines to my bureau. When I get home, I pour out my pockets and place each item in its outline. This allowed me to save time looking for my keys, wallet, planner, etc.

Find what work best for you. I can only describe what worked for me in the hopes you will get some ideas. I have a daily checklist I review every morning. I had to create the most efficient order to my routine, because every second matters. Too often I would forget to brush my teeth before I had my tie on, or forget to put on deodorant before I tucked my shirt, or I would tie my tie after I tucked in my pants. Sweat the small stuff; it will make everything else easier.

CHAPTER VII
STYLE

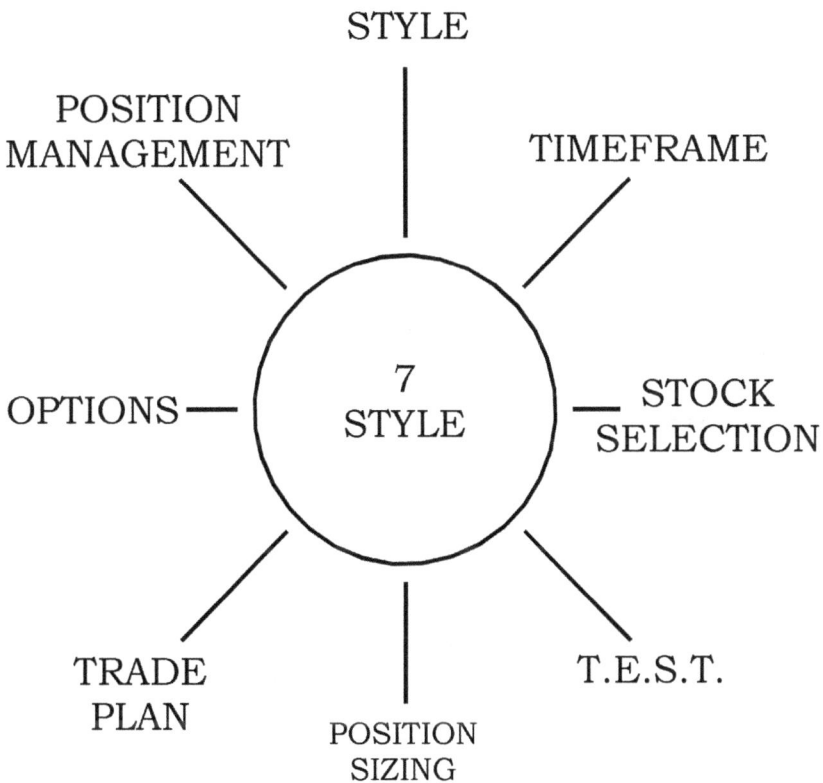

Which **style** fits your personality?

I realize what works for me, may not work for you. I'm going to go over short and long-term time-frames to spark a flash that lights up your mind and reveals something that, perhaps, you didn't know was there.

Your **timeframe**...

Think of the market as having a heartbeat.

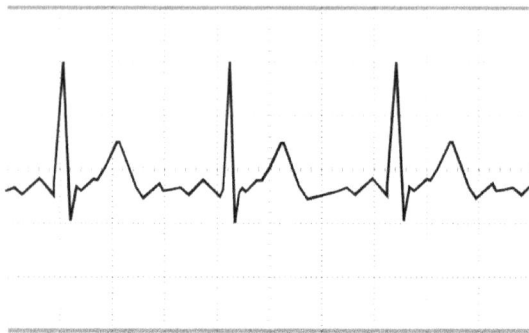

It's all about finding a rhythm you can understand. Timing is EVERYTHING.

The element of time is the first hurdle to clear in finding your rhythm. Stick with a timeframe in which you can identify clear patterns and react with complete ease.

There are many very successful traders and they all have very similar ways to pattern trade using specific timeframes.

Money *flows*, so think of an ocean wave. Note the sine wave patterns. There are two separate waves in the next figure. One long, one short.

The smaller pattern with a smaller sine wave is generally following a longer wave pattern.

Think of the shorter sine waves as ripples on the profile of a water surface. You will see similar 'ripples' in the market, which are needed for the market to balance the buying and selling, or supply and demand.

The smaller waves together form the bigger waves. In the figure, there are three to four shorter waves between every big wave's peak or valley.

I'm going to show you different timeframes, longer - term and shorter-term, to show you the possibilities. You can decide which ONE fits *your* style. I'll start with the longer-term, and then zoom in to show how the two mesh together.

Think of zooming in to each timeframe as looking through a microscope to examine the timeframe at each different zoom.

The first timeframe is the daily chart, which I title as ZoomX1. For all intents and purposes, the daily chart is unmagnified. Second, you will see a 15-minute chart with a magnification X26. Finally, on the five-minute chart you will see a zoom of X78.

The daily chart (Zoom X1)

Each candle represents one day on the daily chart. This chart is showing a +60% on this specific day, and you can tell from the volume bar below the candle, there was high relative volume.

Daily chart with Bollinger bands

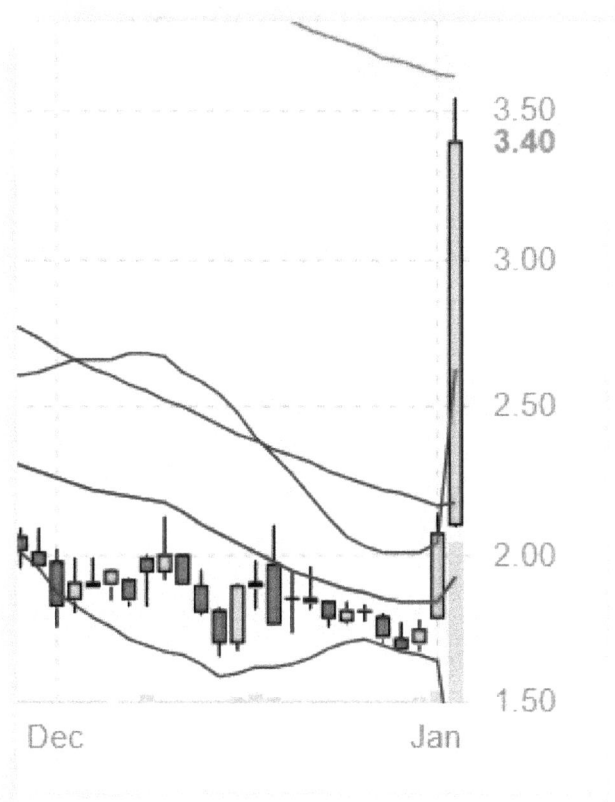

Without the Bollinger bands, the chart may look wide open. These reference lines can be a good indication of future price action. This is where we take a magnifying glass to the *short-term* time frame.

15-minute Chart (Zoom X26)

Same date, same company, different timeframe

This is the same company's *15-minute* chart at the same slice of time, so you only see the movement over the last couple of days instead of the last month.

5-minute Chart (Zoom X78)
Same date, same company, different timeframe

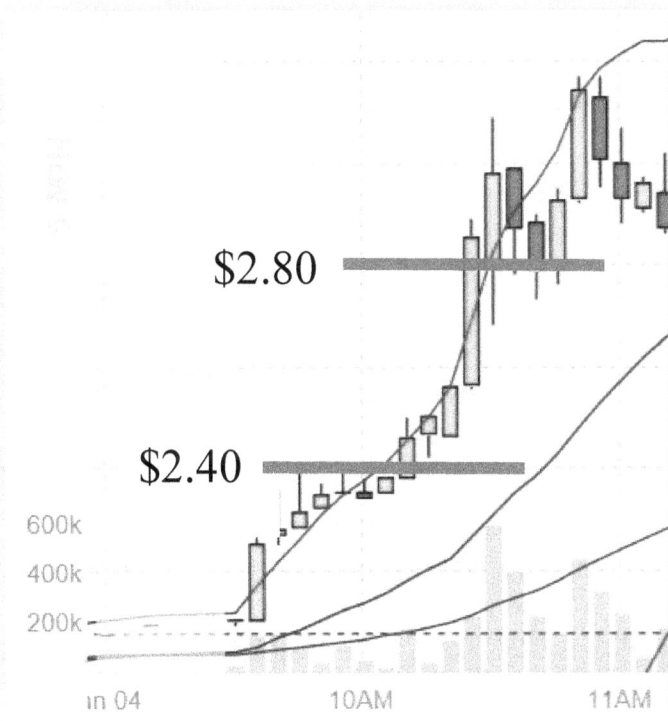

Twenty minutes after breaking $2.40, the price broke $2.80. That's over 16%. Same patterns, different time frames. Because the

Bollinger bands are based on the *period* intervals (i.e. 5-min, 15-min, one day) they will appear different in each timeframe.

These moves happen every day. The idea is to wait for the best-looking setup with the most potential. There may only be a handful of great opportunities any given day. Some days there may not be any. In my experience, I can find at least one solid trade four out of five market days. Don't worry, I'll show you where to look.

JMT
  ⊕ *Better things await you tomorrow*

Volatility is a trading term used to gauge how rapid or unpredictable a price movement. The best *short-*

term traders stick to small caps because of the higher volatility. Although past performance is not indicative of future performance, past volatility is accepted as a reliable indicator of future volatility.

Volatility varies with company size, also known as market capitalization (Cap).

Cap Size	Small	Mid	Large
# of Co.'s*	3,121	1,066	615
Volatility (wk.)*	4.43%	1.93%	1.37%

*As of 2017

Small caps in the table represent companies less than two billion market cap. Mid-sized caps are between two and ten billion. Large are over ten billion.

The market capitalization is the company share price multiplied by the outstanding shares. Think of the outstanding shares as the supply. The buying pressure is the demand, which can be measured by buying volume.

(Share price) x (outstanding shares) = market cap

Because there are 3,121 small cap companies, and only 252 trading days a year, on any given day you can expect a handful of companies to have a record day, breaking market news, company announcements, or company earnings.

Most trading days there are stocks that move 30% or more. These moves are not instantaneous for the most part. They happen throughout the day over short time periods. There are opportune moments, with clear patterns and indicators, right before explosive moves higher, where you can share in the returns with little risk.

Stock Selection for *longer-term* trades...

You can analyze the movements of daily patterns on the weekends or at night and view the *six-month* timeframe, looking for the exact same candlestick patterns you would as if they were five minute candles. Holding positions for weeks and months is known as *position* trading.

There are major differences in stock selection and trade

management when going from shorter-term trading to position trading. One major difference is the screening parameters. You don't want any of your positions to fall apart while holding them, so you choose the most reliable companies. Here are the parameters I use for position trading.

Market Cap above 10 Billion
Volume above 2 Million per day
Price of security above $30
Optionable

This is the exact screen I use to update the Leaderboard on my website, www.theinflectionpt.com. I simply sort by yearly performance and display the top ten stocks. I have faith the outperformers will continue to outperform, all months except January.

The top 10% of stocks outperform the market from February to December, and the only month they don't is January.[J] Refer back to the January effect in _Intel_.

The same basic chart patterns that drive entries and exits in the five-minute timeframe, drive entries and exits on the daily timeframe. How do you manage risk in longer-term trades? Very similarly to how you manage risk in the shorter-term timeframe. You wait until the risk-to-reward is at least two-to-one on the _six-month_ chart.

Check out TIP100's "How to get to first base" to see the golden rule in action. The difference between your entrance price and your stop-loss price is the amount you are

[J]Jagadeesh & Titman, Momentum, 2001

risking. Define your risk pre-trade, just like you would a shorter-term trade.

You need a strategy so you know when to cut your losses objectively.

Market **T.E.S.T.** your plan...

Timeframe	
Entrance	
Stop-loss	
Target	

Your stop-loss is key to defining your risk.

Here's what a T.E.S.T. looks like.

TICKER	FB
TIMEFRAME	1 month
ENTRANCE	$100
STOPLOSS	$95
TARGET	$110

Your entrance, $100, minus your stop-loss, $95, is your risk per share, $5. If you were buying 100 shares, your risk is $5 x 100 = $500.

Shorter-term trading...

Some of the best shorter-term traders I know use four criteria or more to screen stocks for a hot shorter-time trade list. The first is *average volume*.

Average Volume	Over 50K ⌄

This filters out extremely low-volume stocks. The bid (price you can sell at) and ask (price you can buy at) range is wider on stocks that aren't traded often.

Float Short	Low (<5%) ⌄

Float is the number of shares available to trade. Float short is the *short* interest in the stock. Only traders betting a stock price will fall have *short* positions. Float is the supply. When the demand is high, prices increase. When demand is high and supply is low, prices can skyrocket.

Relative Volume	Over 3 ⌄

Screening based on high relative volume helps find stocks experiencing extremes. This will filter out most stocks, because most stocks aren't experiencing extremes. *Extreme* is rare by nature.

Price	Under $10 ⌄

And the last screen is price under $10. Stocks under $10 - and especially stocks under $1 - are riskier. With greater risk comes greater *potential* reward. Stocks with a lower share price tend to have higher percentage moves.

Wait for the best possible setup. There may be some days when the right move is to not make any trades. This is one of the hardest situations to recognize because doing nothing may be unfulfilling. After finding the best possible candidate of the day, you take the trade to your patented checklist.

Here is the *short-term* checklist...

- ✓ Enter trade into TIP's Trade Template as seen on TIP100
- ✓ News catalyst or event
- ✓ Extreme prices
- ✓ Relatively high volume
- ✓ Low float
- ✓ Less than 100 million shares outstanding
- ✓ Price breakout
- ✓ Former runner
- ✓ Reward double the risk
- ✓ Enter at nine-period moving average
- ✓ Enter OCO order after entry

The first thing to remember is to write down your trade and enter it into my spreadsheet to calculate your risk vs. reward. Ideally, you want a stock that has great breaking news, is experiencing extreme prices, with high relative volume, low float, a clear price breakout, and a history of previous runs higher.

Short-term trading requires making decisions in minutes. Exercising the mind *and* body before short-term trading is recommended to increase alertness. Also, as little as 2% dehydration may cause a breakdown of your basic math skills. You are most dehydrated in the morning, because you lose about a pound and a half of water weight overnight. Drink some water!

When beginning, try sticking to one or two positions at a time, so you can manage your *risk* appropriately. You want full control of yourself and your position. One-fifth of your performance has nothing to do with what your positions are, and everything to do with how you manage your positions.

Short-term trading may be appealing for those seeking employment or financial freedom. The *shorter-term* timeframe becomes less risky as you only enter stocks with exploding price movements.

When you learn to sense that perfect scenario, you'll realize it usually doesn't last for more than fifteen to twenty minutes. Stagnant or bleeding positions should get cut fast, like five minutes fast. If the move doesn't happen right away, the probability of it happening at all plummets.

1%

2%

3%

Position sizing...

The ONE thing that costs ONE in three Service Members 90% or more...

The ONE thing that can save one in three Service Members 90% of his or her money is a key piece of trading performance known as *Position Sizing*. To lose 90%, you must risk 90% or more.

Reducing your position sizing in any one area helps to avoid the catastrophic loss. Think of lowering your position sizing as army crawling instead of standing up. Keeping a low profile increases your odds of survival. You're not as exposed. Cash is a good position too.

Consistency comes after you can risk the same amount on each trade. I lost faith early on because I was losing money risking too much per trade, or not bothering to plan for the worst-case scenario. I risked huge percentages of my account balance, and took massive losses.

Beginning to trade, just like beginning anything, you should accept that you aren't likely to be good at it right away. Becoming good at trading, like becoming good at anything else, takes practice. Lowering your risk per trade is the first defense to limiting massive losses. All traders have a win-loss percentage per trade over a given timeframe. Not all traders track it.

Even with a win-loss percentage of 55% winning trades to 45% losing ones, looking at a 50-trade period, statistically you have a 31.3% chance of losing six straight trades in a row. If your risk per trade is 1%, there is about one in three chance you would be down 6% after six trades.

If your risk per trade is 10%, there is about a one in three chance of losing 60% after six trades. Coming back from a 60% loss would require you to gain 150% just to get back to even. Coming back from a 6% loss would only require a 6.4% gain to breakeven.

Controlling your position sizing will help set you apart from the average traders. It will also narrow down areas of improvement or flaws in your plan. Your first problem may be that you don't have enough winning trades when compared to your total trades.

In Dale Carnegie's book, *How to Win Friends and Influence People*, there is a story about Theodore Roosevelt. Roosevelt proclaimed 'If you could guarantee you are right 55% of the time, you can go to Wall Street and make one million a day.' This was written over seventy-five years ago, and I believe it still holds true.

If you don't track your win-loss percentage, you will not have a point of reference to set your expectations. Some traders collect big checks like lottery winners. The difference is there is no luck involved. They have perfected their strategy, position sizing, position management, trading style and stock selection. Here is an excerpt from my first book, The Inflection Point: *Where Trading Meets Investing* ™.

The year was 1987, and Larry Williams set out to make history. Larry entered the World Cup of Traders to prove his personal method was not only effective, but that it was the best. The competition lets traders compete to track who can gain the most money in one year, starting with $10,000 dollars. One of Larry's advantages was he studied the Commitment of Trader's (COT) reports released by the

Commodity Futures Trading Commission (CFTC). Volumes of Long (Buying) and Short (Selling) positions for common commodities are released to the public weekly. More importantly, this report separates the Commercial Institutions and Hedge Funds, new positions from the Non-commercial and Unreported buying and selling. The Non-commercial traders aren't as important to follow as the Commercials. The Commercials are buying and selling to lower their risk because their business is at risk.

If there is a large movement in a commodity price, followed sharply by an increase in buying or selling volume from the Commercials, it may be wise to take interest and trade with the Commercials, which was part of Larry's trade plan. At the twelve-month mark when the World Cup of Traders competition ended, Larry achieved net gains of 11,376%.

The next highest return since the tournament's inception was not within 10,000%. That's a difference of over ONE MILLION dollars all in one year. The market condition in 1987 had everything to do with his returns, but the returns had everything to do with his tactics.

Ten years later, his daughter won the same contest and finished up 1,000% at the 12-month mark. Larry claims to have made millions multiple times trading, and there is every reason to believe his claim.

Form your **trade plan**…

Your plan should contain all the safeguards to prohibit trading based on your feelings. You must *feel* when the *desire* to trade is based on fear or greed, and counter with reflection of those emotions. Exercise patience. Say to yourself, "I am feeling greedy," or "I am feeling excited." These are natural human emotions that are aroused by money. Take a step back and remember you need to be a strategist to win long-term. Suppress the desire, and trade objectively based on your plan.

It took hard work and discipline for me to get there and it's an ongoing process. I battle emotions daily, as I'm sure all of you do. I know I can help you overcome your biggest challenges. Email me, or call me and leave a message. I'm here for you.

If you have ever attempted trading, you absolutely have experienced the emotions of a fluctuating account balance. Having a process with built in guidelines, checklists, and triggers can help break those feelings and enable you to analyze your risks objectively.

Do you realize what makes up your performance basis?

Your trade style, position sizing, position management, stock selection style, and options strategy selection all contribute to your performance. Some may have a bigger impact than others depending on your style of trading.

YOUR PERFORMANCE BASIS

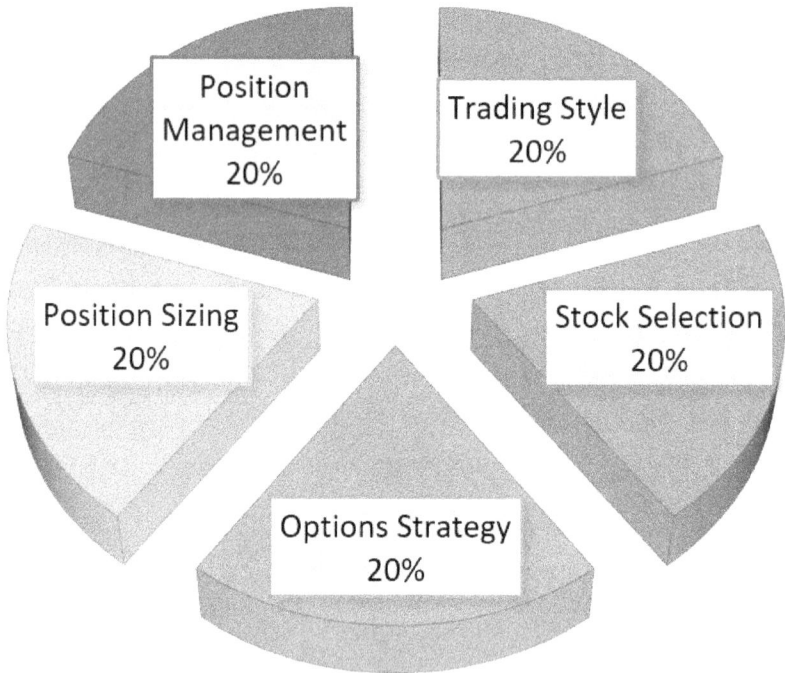

Position Management 20%

Trading Style 20%

Position Sizing 20%

Stock Selection 20%

Options Strategy 20%

Your **options** are endless...

Options can be bought and sold just like stock. However, if you can't make money buying and selling stock, buying and selling options will just make your problems worse.

I'll shine some light onto the options world to merely show you that your trading opportunities really are endless.

There are two types of options. The call option is a contract that gives you the right to buy 100 shares.

The put option is a contract that gives you the right to sell 100 shares. Not all companies have options, and most of the small ones don't. The companies that aren't heavily traded are the worst companies from which to buy and sell options. It would cost you too much to get into and out of the position.

Call option (right to buy 100 shares)

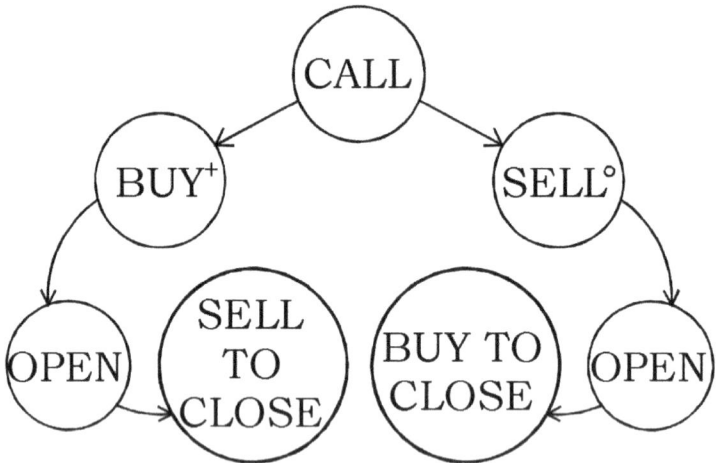

$^+$RIGHT TO BUY   OBLIGATION$^°$ TO DELIVER

A call option is a contract to buy 100 shares at a specific price before the expiration date. The contract price is known as the strike price. You can buy a call option or sell a call option. When you *buy* a call, you have the right to buy the shares. When you *sell* a call, you have the obligation to deliver 100 shares.

Put option (right to sell 100 shares)

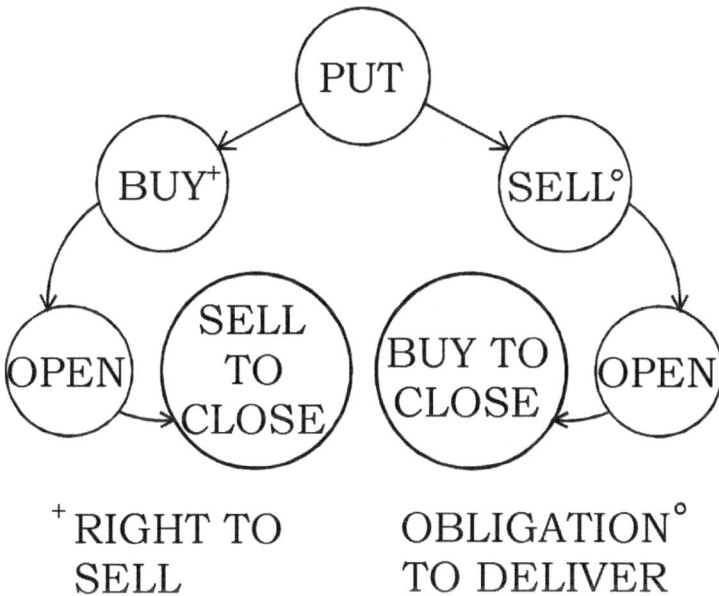

⁺RIGHT TO SELL OBLIGATION° TO DELIVER

A put option is a contract to sell 100 shares at the contract price before the expiration date. The contract price is known as the strike. You can buy a put option or sell a put option. When you *buy* a put, you have the right to sell the shares. When you *sell* a put, you have the obligation to deliver 100 shares.

The obligation to deliver may be called at any time, because it is an obligation. Just as when you have the right to buy, you can exercise your right at any time. When you exercise the contract, you will get 100 shares added to your account. When a put option is exercised, you will be short 100 shares. You sold something you don't have.

Selling something you don't have is called being *short* shares. If the underlying price of the security skyrockets, your broker may close your position at the market price. The broker is in control and has the right to close a *short* position. You will owe the broker the difference between the market price when you bought the short, and the market price when your broker closes the position.

I point this out because I've seen many beginner traders blow up their real money account by ignoring this risk and not setting a stop-loss on their short position. One trader literally left a position open while he went out to lunch, and lost $50,000, which was his whole account balance. Beware of what might happen if you ignore your risk.

JMT

⊕ *You don't own positions in which you don't fully understand your risk*

Don't buy or sell anything without properly protecting your position with stop-loss orders or positioning yourself to accept the maximum possible loss.

Your performance will be 20% reflective of your trading strategy...

Your trading strategy needs to be well tested so you can discover where you're going right and where you're going wrong. This can be translated to any field of business. These concepts are universal to buying and selling anything.

Define your Strategy.

> *What* hours will you dedicate?
> *When* are you going to plan your trades?
> *When* will you execute the orders?
> *Where* will you find space to operate or execute?
> *What* is your timeframe?
> *What* type of vehicles will you use?

Leave nothing to chance.

You need to set aside your happy place, where your friends and family know not to interrupt you while finding your vehicle. Just like *Happy Gilmore* found his happy place before sending in the game-winning putt slash chip shot to silence Shooter McGavin.

Position Management...

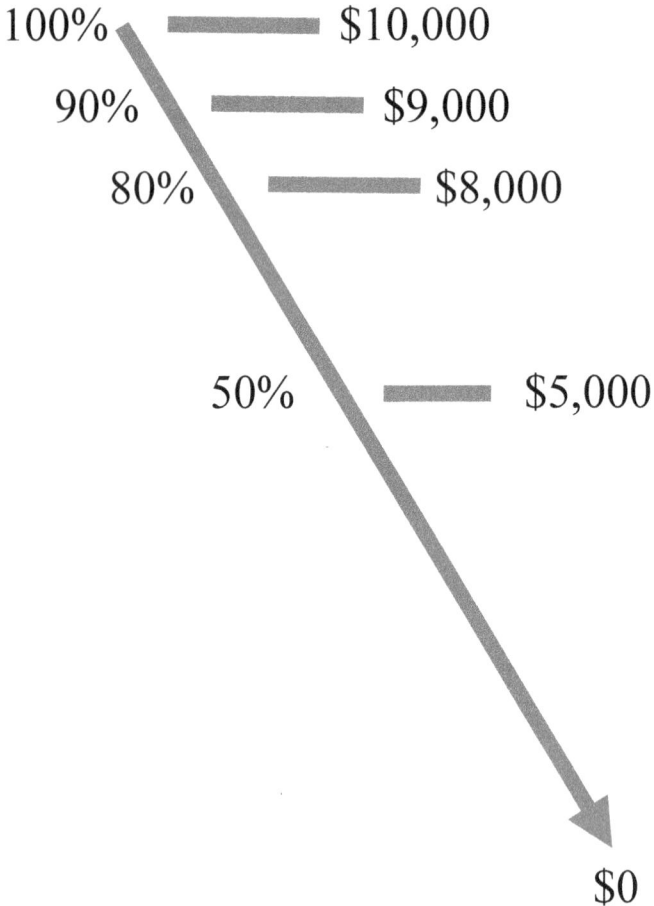

100% ▬▬▬▬▬ $10,000
90% ▬▬▬▬ $9,000
80% ▬▬▬▬ $8,000

50% ▬▬▬ $5,000

$0

Keeping money in any position other than cash, there is a real risk it may go to zero. When buying and selling stock in your market, a stop-loss may be used to protect yourself, with one exception.

If you plan to hold something forever, and continuously invest in a position, a stop-loss will not be necessary. I personally feel like this type of investment should be reserved for your main vehicle or a well-known one, very solidly positioned, and one that you have faith will stand the test of time. Don't get married to one position, unless this is *the* one.

For the record, Warren Buffet advises a portfolio comprised of 10% in short-term government bonds and 90% in a very low cost S&P 500 Index fund (he suggests Vanguard's, VFINX).

CHAPTER VIII
PERSONAL COURAGE

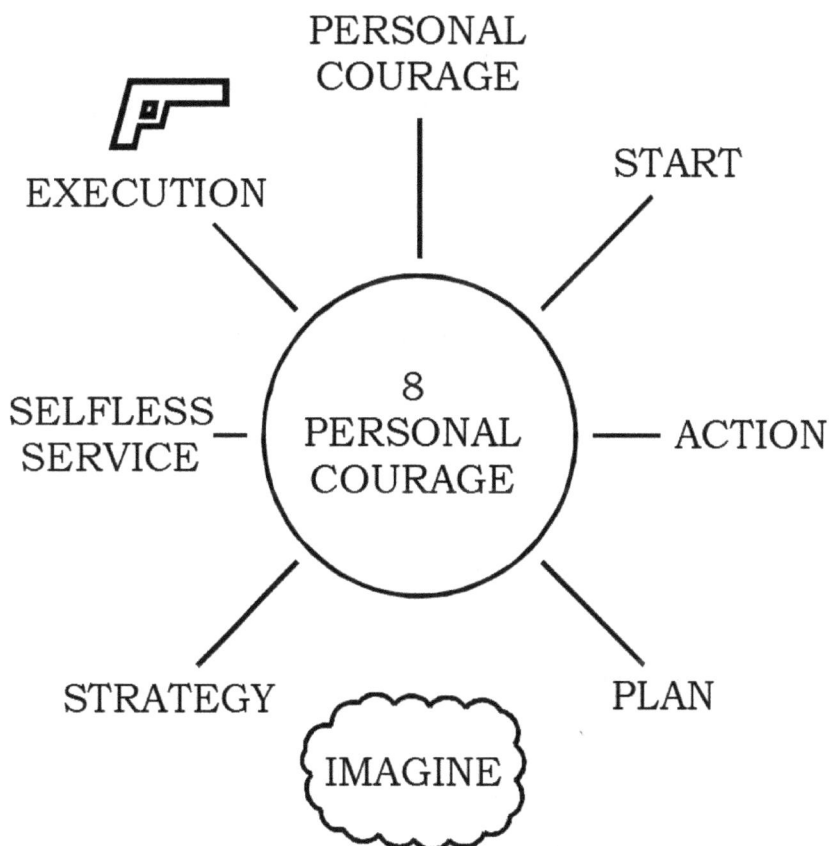

PERSONAL
COURAGE

START

EXECUTION

8
PERSONAL
COURAGE

SELFLESS
SERVICE

ACTION

STRATEGY

PLAN

IMAGINE

You now have **Personal Courage**…

Just do it. Simulate your market as best you can and find ways to test your plan with little to no risk. Volunteer for your biggest fear. Stand up and embrace your audience. After strategizing with techniques from _Style_ about patterns from _Intel_, you're prepared to market-test your plan.

You will have your own unique experience in your market, just as another Service Member's experience will be unique to him or her.

If you have had any experience at all in the market, you probably have had some bad experiences. One in three who tries to actively manage positions loses everything or close to it. I love to point out that I was no different. When I started out, I lost a significant amount of REAL money. It didn't occur to me that I should practice first. I couldn't see the benefits of trading in a simulated market. Why waste my REAL time with FAKE money? This is what I used to think.

I thought I knew. Now, I don't think I know; I know I think. Only one in a thousand can *think* so clearly as to act out even a fraction of their imagination with perfect execution. Only one in a thousand can *see* more than a fraction of what passes before their eyes daily. When you can both *see* with perfect vision and *think* with vivid imagination, you are one in a million. It's this mastery level that allows you to own your own cow and milk it.

Throughout my experiences in the market, my *strategy* has changed significantly. I admit that I was wrong. I had a terrible strategy, especially at first. It didn't get better overnight either. To admit that you're wrong is only admitting that you are wiser today than you were yesterday. If you keep doing what you've always done, you will get what you always got.

Do you think it felt good to lose a good chunk of my hard-earned cash? Well, it didn't. In fact, that upset feeling in my stomach that I still *feel* anytime I *think* about those losses is one of my major driving forces. I used that feeling to discover a systematic approach to profit 30% every year by qualifying trades with checklists and calculating my risk pre-trade.

Here's the thing: no one is going to believe you can do this at first. You need to show you can do it with a fake $100,000. If you can't do it with fake money, you have no business attempting it with real money. Even when you can do it on paper, this doesn't mean you will be able to control your emotions the same way when real money is involved.

Start...

It is true that if you never start, you will never fail. Remember Homer Simpson, *"Trying* is the first step toward failure!"? Trying *is* the first step toward failure.

If you are having trouble starting, start with *Desire*. Start with what you really want and create your plan. Execute the plan then tweak it to make it better. You don't need to spend any money to start. You can start by forming ideas in your head using your imagination. Practice role playing or engaging in simulated markets.

Do only what you want to be doing in your free time. Don't hesitate. When you hesitate, your idea gets cold. It doesn't matter where you start, it matters where you end up.

Once you have a clear picture of what you are trying to accomplish, and it feels right, you can move on to action.

Action is turning your thoughts into reality. Thoughts, cleverly stirred with feelings, induce action. Putting pen to paper is a great first action. Complete more actions per day and increase the momentum of your snowball. Don't just do anything; do the *right* thing. Fail fast to learn fast. Your failure rate inevitably increases with actions.

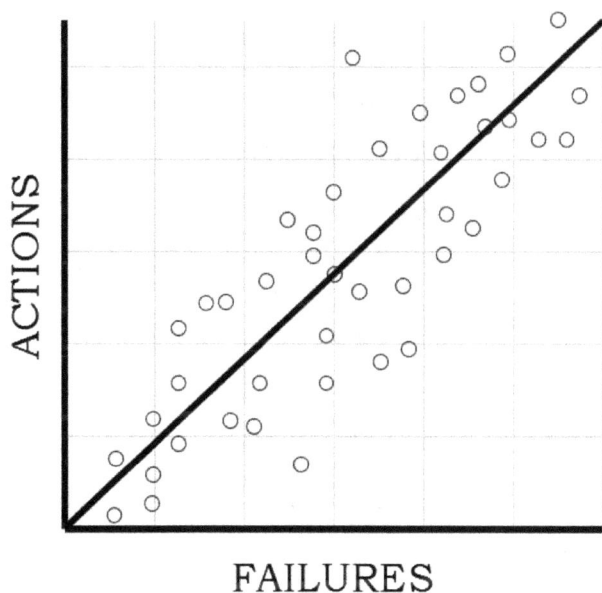

"Every failure is the seed of an equivalent benefit." *~Napoleon Hill*

When a reporter asked Thomas Edison "How did it feel to fail 1,000 times?" he famously answered "I didn't fail 1,000 times; the light bulb was an invention of 1,000 steps."

There will inevitably be losses and failures on the road to your one major desire. Only those who learn from their failures will become successful. When you fail, there is always a reason. Take note of important details to avoid repeating mistakes. Teach your lessons to those who stand to benefit the most. Extend the olive branch, especially if you see a Service Member drowning.

Failure to the point of exhaustion is not good. It's important to recognize exhaustion and realize that little amount of power left in your tank is best spent tomorrow. Rest your mind. Take time to recover.

When you wake up, revise your **plan** for the better...

Even this book was written and re-written countless times even before my editor saw it. Most admired authors in history created their best works with the help of an editor. I know this book wouldn't be half of what it is without my amazing editor. Thank you Jill! Don't be afraid to approach a mentor with an open mind about your work.

Spark some long-term thinking about where you really want to be in ten years. How do you see your business growing?

Establish deep roots so that you aren't blown over by the next hurricane to shake up your market.

Alternative plans can be distracting. Concentrate efforts on your one major desire. Only 2% of people even know what their one major desire is. Hopefully you do now that you're this far along, and if you don't, you will tomorrow.

It helps to **imagine**...

Thoughts are real things. At the first Annual Shareholder Meeting for The Inflection Point Inc. I asked everyone to imagine Abe Lincoln standing right next to me saying, "That some may achieve great success, is proof we all may achieve great success." The fact that there are billionaires in this world means that you or I may become one. You can even lose one billion dollars and still become the President of the United States.

Just because something isn't real, doesn't mean you can't make it real.

If I believe the spirit of Lincoln is with me, which I do, no one can deny the REAL impact it has on my actions. Sure, not all the shareholders at my meeting saw Lincoln. I didn't expect everyone to see him. I thought maybe one out of the twenty-two members might *feel* his presence.

Strategy...

I start out promising there is a way to make 30% profit working part-time and remotely from anywhere, with low to no overhead, and the highest growth potential of any industry. And there is. But don't expect it to happen overnight. It takes time and effort to master any valuable skill. The time spent must be continuous and progressive, similar to _Organization_.

The good news is, you don't need to master _Self Control_ to immediately see some beautiful benefits. Just knowing _the right_ things to do can be a weight off.

You need to match your _Style_ to your personality. Use _Intel_ to tactically execute your strategy with _Desire_.

There is no profession with a greater growth potential than that of a _tactical and strategic_ trader; however it's your _Team_ that makes you.

There is nothing more dangerous in this world than only thinking about you.

Now go in with the right mindset and execute. Build up your _Self Confidence_, know you're worth well over a million dollars in earnings potential, and do it. Ignore everyone that isn't helping.

Young or old, invest time in *your* passion whether it's a job, hobby, or leisure activity right now. The oak sleeps in the acorn: it's time to become the mighty oak.

Selfless Service...

Jack Nadel is one of the great mentors I found by subscribing to Thrive15.com. This is the one source recommended by Lee Cockerell that I referenced back in the *Team* chapter. Subscriptions are free for Military and Veterans.

"When I reflect on all of my life experiences, it becomes clear that when you help others, you are actually helping yourself. The material assistance you give your neighbors and associates will be repaid in many unexpected and fulfilling ways." – Jack Nadel, from *The Evolution of an Entrepreneur*

Now, **Execute**…

Once you learn these wealth creation skills, no one can ever take them from you. You can take these skills anywhere you want to go, and upon mastery of the skills, you can go anywhere you desire.

NOW HIRING...
<u>MILITARY SUPERSTARS</u>!!!

Be your own boss.

Experience financial freedom.

Work part-time and remotely from anywhere with an internet connection.

Make 30% profit *or more* every year.

Create your vehicle in any market with low to no startup cost or overhead.

Control your own destiny.

Send paper and video resumes to...

<u>info@theinflectionpt.com</u>

For those suffering from depression or Post Traumatic Stress Disorder, please don't hesitate to reach out and give me a call.

856-685-4681

Please leave a message, and I will get back to you as soon as humanly possible.

Also, www.ptsd.va.gov is a great resource:

FOR IMMEDIATE ASSISTANCE IN A CRISIS

1-800-273-8255

In loving memory of

Stephanie Marchesani

About the Author

David Koper committed to assist the United States Army Corps of Engineers (USACE) by deploying to Afghanistan for six months from Sep 2011 to Mar 2012, and then seven months from Dec 2012 to June 2013. His reasons for deploying included two things: God and Country.

In theatre, Koper grew an affinity for the United States Armed Forces whose job it was to protect him. Security forces escorted him into and out of local Afghan communities as the Corps of Engineers tasked Koper with contract oversight on critical missions. Projects included pre-stressed bridge reconstruction in the Kapisa Province and construction oversight of Afghan Police Headquarters outside of Bagram Air Field.

While Service Members risked their lives to protect the USACE Engineer, Koper felt the desire to give something back that would improve the quality of life for all Service Members overseas. Knowing internet access is limited, and activities outside work scarce, Koper founded The Inflection Point Inc. and developed *Create Wealth While Serving Your Country.*

www.ingramcontent.com/pod-product-compliance
Lightning Source LLC
Chambersburg PA
CBHW060012210326
41520CB00009B/865